OVER 15,000 WORDS

The Scholastic Dictionary of

SPELLING

Marvin Terban

SCHOLASTIC
REFERENCE

For Karen and Jennifer, because you really need this book

Book design: Nancy Sabato
Composition: Kevin Callahan
Illustrations: Harry Campbell

Library of Congress Cataloging-in-Publication Data

Terban, Marvin
      Scholastic dictionary of spelling / Marvin Terban
         p. cm.
      ISBN 0-590-30697-9
      1. Spellers. 2. English language—Orthography and spelling. I. Title.
PE1146.T38 1998   97-18020
428.1—dc21   CIP
                                                                 AC

12 11 10 9 8 7 6 5 4 3 2 1   8 9/9 0/0 01 02

Printed in the U.S.A.   09
First printing, February 1998

Introduction

Someone writes something. Other people read and understand it. That's good communication.

Someone writes something. Other people have trouble reading it. They misunderstand. That's poor communication.

The trouble can be that the letters are too small or the ink is too light or the writing is too mezzy. But very often the trouble is the spelling.

When your spelling is bad, it will take more time and effort for people to understand what you are trying to say. Bad spelling is confusing and perplexing and befuddling and frustrating and annoying—and embarrassing to the writer. So it's really important to spell as many words as possible as correctly as possible. That way, you'll get your meaning across, avoid misunderstandings, and save yourself from embarrassment.

English is a very tricky language with many, many words. According to some word experts, French has about 100,000 words, Russian has 135,000, and German has 185,000. But English has over 600,000 words! English is made up of words from about 100 other languages, so no wonder English spelling is so full of exceptions, irregularities, peculiarities, and just plain confusing words. It's not your fault English words are so hard to spell—but you should try your best to spell them right, just the same.

This book will help a lot, so keep it nearby when you write.

HOW TO LOOK UP A WORD

Luckily, many words in English are spelled just about the way they sound. Since all the words in this book are listed in alphabetical order, the way the beginning of a word is spelled is very important. Finding a word will be easier if you can get the first few letters right.

Slowly say the word you're trying to spell. (Say the word aloud if you can.) Think about what the first letter might be. Turn to the section of this dictionary that lists words that begin with that letter. (Use the large letters printed in the top corners of the pages to help you flip to the right section quickly.) Next, think about the first syllable. How do you think that could be spelled?

GUIDE WORDS

If you think you know the first few letters of a word, check them against the guide words in large print at the tops of the pages. Ask yourself: Is the word I'm looking for between these two guide words according to its alphabetical order?

For example, let's say you have to spell *cranberry, corporal,* and *criticize.* The guide words at the top of one page are *counselor* and *crazy. Cranberry* will be on that page, but *corporal* will be on an earlier page and *criticize* will be on a later page. That's because in alphabetical order, the words go: *corporal, counselor, cranberry, crazy, criticize.*

SYLLABLES

This dictionary breaks words into syllables as they are pronounced. The accented syllable (the one you pronounce a little more strongly) is printed in **boldface** type.

Sometimes words are accented differently, depending on how they are used in a sentence. For example, the word *permit* is pronounced **per**•mit as a noun (Here's my fishing **per**mit) and per•**mit** as a verb (I can't per**mit** you to do that). In this book, you will find the part of speech (noun, verb, adjective) of these especially tricky words abbreviated in parentheses (n., v., adj.).

SCAN

Once you think you know the first few letters, sound out the rest of the word to try to figure out the rest of the letters. Even if you are not sure which letters come in the middle and at the end, you can still probably find the word if you get the beginning right and then scan the lists. Look quickly up and down the columns. Sometimes you'll be able to spot the word as your eye travels on the page.

Please note that this special spelling dictionary is different from other dictionaries. Other books put words together that are related. The plural of a noun will come right after the singular, and other forms of a verb will come right after the present tense. But this dictionary lists all words in strict alphabetical order. For instance, *ladies* (plural noun) comes before *lady* (singular noun), and *carried* (the past tense of the verb) comes before *carry* (the present tense). So make sure that you scan both up and down the lists.

CONFUSING SOUNDS

Suppose you look up a word the way it sounds to you and you can't find it. Here are some suggestions.

If the word begins with a consonant sound

The consonant sounds are usually spelled as you might expect them to be. But sometimes a consonant sound can be spelled more than one way at the beginning of a word:

The **f** sound can be spelled with **f** (**f**abulous **f**un) or **ph** (**ph**araoh, **ph**easant).

The hard **g** sound can be spelled with **g** (**g**ame, **g**arden) or with **gh** (**gh**etto, **gh**ost).

The **j** sound can be spelled with **j** (**j**am, **j**elly) or with **g** (**g**iant, **g**ym).

The **k** sound can be spelled with **k** (**k**arate, **k**itchen), with **c** (**c**at, **c**omb), or with **ch** (**ch**lorine, **ch**orus).

The **n** sound can be spelled with **n** (**n**aughty, **n**ice), with **kn** (**kn**ee, **kn**ife, **kn**ot), with **gn** (**gn**ash, **gn**ome), or with **pn** (**pn**eumonia, **pn**eumatic).

The **r** sound can be spelled with **r** (**r**ascal, **r**eceive, **r**igmarole), with **wr** (**wr**angle, **wr**ench, **wr**iggle), or with **rh** (**rh**inoceros, **rh**ubarb, **rh**ythm).

The **s** sound can be spelled with **s** (**s**arcastic, **s**ecretary), with **c** (**c**ement, **c**inema, **c**yclone), with **sc** (**sc**issors, **sc**enery, **sc**epter), or with **ps** (**ps**alm, **ps**ychiatrist).

The **t** sound can be spelled with **t** (**t**ackle, **t**oadstool) or with **pt** (**pt**erodactyl, **pt**omaine).

The **w** sound can be spelled with **w** (**w**izard, **w**obble) or with **wh** (**wh**ale, **wh**imper).

The **z** sound can be spelled, with **z** (**z**any, **z**ombie) or with **x** (**X**erox, **x**ylophone).

Blends

Two or three consonants sometimes work together to form one sound at the beginning of a word, such as **sc** in **sc**are or **str** in **str**ong. Say **strong** aloud slowly. Do you hear the blend of letters? **s**. . . **t**. . . **r**. . . ong.

Sometimes the blends can have tricky spellings at the beginning of a word:

The **sh** sound can be spelled with **sh** (**sh**ark, **sh**epherd, **sh**iver), with **s** (**s**urely, **s**ugary), or with **ch** (**ch**ef, **ch**amois, **ch**arade).

The **sk** sound can be spelled with **sk** (**sk**ateboard, **sk**edaddle, **sk**ull), with **sc** (**sc**alpel, **sc**arecrow), with **sch** (**sch**edule, **sch**olar), or with **squ** (**squ**are, **squ**irrel, **squ**irt).

The **kr** sound can be spelled with **kr** (**Kr**emlin, **kr**ypton), with **cr** (**cr**y, **cr**eep, **cr**ocodile), or with **chr** (**Chr**istmas, **chr**omosome).

Make sure to think about all the letters in the blend before you start to look for the word.

Silent letters

Sometimes there are letters that make no sound at all at the beginning of a word, but you still have to put them in to spell the word right.

The letter **p** may be silent when it's followed by an **s** (as in **ps**ychic or **ps**eudonym) or by a **t** (as in **pt**armigan or **pt**erodactyl).

When the consonants **gn**, **kn**, and **wr** are written together, the first letter is silent (as in **gn**at, **kn**ot, and **wr**ote).

H is sometimes silent (as in **h**erb and **h**onest). The sound of the word starts with the sound of the vowel that follows the **h**.

If the word begins with a vowel . . .

Vowels have these sounds:

- a can sound like the *a* in *apple, able, always, alone*
- e can sound like the *e* in *elephant, equal, effect*
- i can sound like the *i* in *inch* or *idea*
- o can sound like the *o* in *olive, ocean,* or *other*
- u can sound like the *u* in *up* or *unit*

Because many vowels can make the same sound, you may have to look in more than one place in the dictionary to find a tricky vowel.

WHAT ABOUT HOMOPHONES?

Sometimes words that sound alike can be spelled differently and have different meanings. For example, look at the words *they're, there,* and *their*. You might say: "They're there in their house." But how do you know how to spell each homophone when you write the sentence?

In this dictionary, homophones are treated in a special way. Suppose you look up the word *there*. After the word, you will find in parentheses: (sounds like "their" and "they're"). Next, the word *there* will be used in a sentence to show you its meaning. If that's not the meaning you want, you should move up the list to the word *their*. You will find another sample sentence. If that's still not the right choice, you have one more option. You can move down the list to *they're*. Soon you will have the exact spelling of each word you want to use.

Note: Some teachers call homophones "homonyms."

COMPOUNDS

When a word is made up of other words, it is often difficult to decide how to write it. Should the words be written as one word, as in *cheerleader*, or are they divided by a hyphen, as in *old-fashioned*, or are they separated by a space, as in *air force*? This book can show you quickly the way the word should be written.

MORE HELP

Many words follow regular spelling patterns and are not too tough to spell once you know the rules. You'll find "A Dozen and One Spelling Rules" (and a few exceptions) beginning on page 9.

But other words don't follow the regular rules or have really hard spellings. Over time, people have made up tricks to help them remember how to spell these difficult words. You'll find a list of "Memory Tricks" beginning on page 14.

Sometimes it's hard to look up a word in the dictionary because the beginning of the word is not spelled the way you would expect. Words like that are listed in the "Misspeller's Dictionary" beginning on page 212. Turn to this section when all else fails.

No one is born a great speller, but if you work at it, you can get better. Just remember that when you're not 100%, absolutely, positively sure how to spell a word, look it up!

A Dozen and One Spelling Rules

Here are some helpful rules.

ADDING SUFFIXES

1. Don't change the spelling of the root word when you add the suffix **-ly** to any word that doesn't end in **y.**

   Examples:
   sincere + ly = sincerely
   beautiful + ly = beautifully

   Exceptions:
   true + ly = truly
   whole + ly = wholly

2. Don't change the spelling of the root word when you add the suffix **-ness** to any word that does not end in the letter **y.**

   Examples:
   kind + ness = kindness
   rough + ness = roughness

3. Keep the silent **e** at the end of a word when you add a suffix that begins with a **consonant** (like **-m**ent, **-f**ul, and **-l**y).

   Examples:
   arrange + ment = arrang**e**ment
   peace + ful = peac**e**ful
   sincere + ly = sinc**e**rely

   Exceptions:
   acknowledg**e** + ment = acknowled**gm**ent

judg**e** + ment = jud**gm**ent
tru**e** + ly = tru**ly**
whol**e** + ly = who**ll**y

4. Drop the silent **e** at the end of a word when you add a suffix that begins with a **vowel** (such as **-e**d, **-i**ng, **-o**us, **-a**bly, **-a**l, and **-y**).

    Examples:
    hope + ing = hoping
    shine + y = shiny
    fortune + ate = fortunate
    dose + age = dosage
    nature + al = natural
    fame + ous = famous

    Exceptions: notic**ea**ble and courag**eo**us

5. Double the final consonant when the word is just one syllable, the last two letters are **one vowel + one consonant,** and you add a suffix that begins with a vowel (such as **-i**ng, **-e**d, **-e**r, **-e**st, **-a**l, **-y,** etc.).

    Examples:
    swim, swi**mm**ing, swi**mm**er
    drag, dra**gg**ing, dra**gg**ed
    hot, ho**tt**er, ho**tt**est
    rob, ro**bb**ing, ro**bb**er
    flop, flo**pp**y, flo**pp**ing

6. Change the **y** to **i** before adding the suffix when you add the suffixes **-ness**, **-age**, or **-ly** to any word that ends in the letter **y.**

    Examples:
    busy + ness = bus**i**ness

lonely + ness = loneliness
marry + age = marriage
happy + ness = happiness
day + ly = daily

7. Add **ful** not **full** when you add the suffix **-ful** to any word.

Examples:
thought + ful = thoughtful
cheer + ful = cheerful

FORMING PLURALS

8. Just add **s** when a word ends with **o** and there's a **vowel** before the **o**.

Examples:
one rodeo, two rodeos
one radio, two radios

9. Add **es** when a word ends with **o** and there's a **consonant** before the **o**.

Examples:
one tomato, two tomatoes
one torpedo, two torpedoes

Exception: With words that end with **o** and have something to do with **music**, just add **s** to form their **plurals**:
alto, altos
solo, solos
piano, pianos

Note: With the following words, either plural is correct, but the first is preferred: tornados or tornadoes, mosquitos or mosquitoes, dominos or dominoes, halos or haloes, mottos or mottoes, zeros or zeroes.

10. Just add **s** when the word ends with the letter **y** and there is a **vowel** before the **y**.

Examples:
one boy, two boy**s**
one key, two key**s**

11. Change the **y** to **i** and add **es** when the word ends with the letter **y,** and there is a **consonant** before the **y**.

Examples:
one lady, two lad**ies**
one country, two countr**ies**

FORMING COMPOUNDS

12. Don't change the spelling of either word when you want to put **two words together** to form a new compound word.

Examples:
baby + sitter = baby-sitter
teen + age = teenage
shoe + lace = shoelace

If the first word ends with the same letter that the second word begins with, keep both letters in the middle of the new compound word.

Examples:
roo**m** + **m**ate = roo**mm**ate
nigh**t** + **t**ime = nigh**tt**ime

Exception: pas**t** + **t**ime = pastime

Note: Sometimes the compound word will be one word (example: **sand-paper**), two words (example: **high school**), or a word with a hyphen in the middle (example: **custom-made**).

There's no rule for this. If you're not sure which version of your compound word is correct, look it up.

AN OLD RHYME

13. **I** before **e** (or is it **e** before **i**?)

If you know a word has the letters **i** and **e** in it together, but you can't remember which comes first, recite this well-known poem:

I *before* **e**
Except after **c**
Or when sounded like **a**
As in neighbor *and* weigh

That rule will work for most words such as: **achievement, believe, brief, chief, die, grief, lie, pie, retrieve, tie, unwieldy, ceiling, conceit, conceited, conceive, deceit, deceive, perceive, receipt, receive, beige, eighty, freight, neigh, reign, reindeer, sleigh, veil, vein,** and **weight**.

Exceptions: Here are the words that do the *opposite* of the poem: **ancient, being, caffeine, codeine, counterfeit, deficient, efficient, either, financier, foreign, forfeit, heifer, height, heir, kaleidoscope, leisure, neither, protein, scientist, seismologist, seize, sheik, sleight, society, species, stein, sufficient, their, weird**.

Memory Tricks

Trying to spell some words can be very difficult. Sometimes it helps to know a trick or two. Here are some good memory tricks for more than 150 words that are often spelled wrong.

accident
car **c**rash + **dent** = a**cc**i**dent**.

accommodations
At the **c**lean, **c**ute, **m**arvelous **m**otel, the a**ccomm**odations are good.

acre
The cathedral is built on a s**acre**d **acre** of land.

address
ad + **dress** = **address**

advice
My adv**ice** is don't slip on the **ice**.

advise
I ad**vise** you not to catch your finger in the **vise**.

all right
All right is all wrong if it's not *two words*.

altar
The workman got **tar** on the church al**tar**.

alter
She had to al**ter** the **ter**rible gown.

altogether
The **alto** sings **alto**gether lovely songs.

amateur
I, an **amateur**, **am at Eur**ope's shores.

answer
Were you going to give the ans**wer**?

architect
The **arch**itect drew the **arch**.

arctic
The first **c** in ar**c**tic stands for **c**old.

arithmetic
I **met** my arith**met**ic teacher at the mall.

athlete
In the b**ath let e**very **athlete** soak tired muscles.

attendance
at + ten + dance = attendance

autumn
There are **m**any **n**ice events at the end of autu**mn**.

awful
Alligator **w**as **f**eeling **u**nhappy **l**ately. How **awful**!

baggage
Ba**ggage** is lu**ggage**.

balloon
A **ball**oon can be shaped like a **ball**.

banana
This b**anana** is *triple* A quality.

bargain
You can **gain** a lot if you get a bar**gain**.

bazaar

You can **b**uy **a**ncient **z**ebras **and a**musing **r**abbits at a **bazaar**.

beautiful

My **beau** (boyfriend) called me **beau**tiful.

beggar

Did the **beggar beg** in front of the **gar**age?

beginning

The second **inning** is beg**inning**.

behavior

To hit someone with your **vio**lin is bad beha**vio**r.

believe

Don't be**lie**ve a **lie**.

bicycle

It's dangerous to ride a b**icy**cle on an **icy** road.

bookkeeper

This is the only word with three sets of double letters in a row: **oo kk ee**.

brake

For goodness s**ake**, step on the br**ake**!

break

"**Brea**k **brea**d" means to eat.

buoy

This b**uo**y warns ships of **u**nderwater **o**bstacles.

burglar

A bur**glar** doesn't like the **glar**e of a light.

business

bus + **in** + **ess** = **business**

capital

A is the first capit**al** letter of the **al**phabet.

capitol

The dome on the capitol building is round like the **o** in capit**o**l.

captain

On your **cap** there is a s**tain**, **captain**.

cemetery

Do you scream "**e** . . .**e** . . .**e**!" when you go past a c**eme**t**e**ry?

cereal

This ce**real** is made of **real** oats.

chief

"**Hi**," said the c**hi**ef.

chocolate

I was **late**, so I ate all the choco**late**.

choose

Why did the m**oose** ch**oose** a g**oose** with **loose** feathers?

college

There's a **leg** in col**leg**e.

colonel

The **lone** co**lone**l won the battle.

committee

Marvelous **M**ike, **T**errific **T**om, and **E**legant **E**ve are on the co**mmittee**.

compliment

I am grateful for your nice compl**i**ment.

Connecticut

Connect me to **Connect**icut, please.

conscience
In **science** class, we are studying a frog's con**science**.

corps
P.S. The last two letters in cor**ps** are silent.

correspondence
In his **den**, he read his correspon**den**ce.

criticize
Don't critic**ize** the pr**ize**.

dessert
I like **s**omething **s**weet for de**ss**ert.

doctor
If you follow the doct**or**'s **or**ders, you'll get well.

dyeing
Don't leave the **dye in** too long when you're **dyein**g your hair.

eighth
Eighth begins with **eight**.

exaggerate
Good **g**rief! There's a **rat** in exa**gg**era**t**e!

existence
There **is** a **ten** in ex**isten**ce.

extraordinary
This is more than ordinary. It's **extra**ordinary.

February
Cold people say "**br**" in Fe**br**uary.

fiend
Let's put an **end** to this fi**end**.

flammable
Many **m**atches are fla**mm**able.

foreign
The **foreign** man needed a room **for eig**ht **n**ights.

forth
March **fort**h from the **fort**.

forty
The **fort** held out for **fort**y days.

fourth
Four is the **four**th number.

gallon
All I need is a g**all**on.

gnarled
Gee, this is a **nar**row **led**ge to climb with **gnarled** hands.
(Note: The "g" in **gnarled** is silent.)

governor
The **governor** will **govern or** we won't vote for him.

grammar
Don't **mar** (spoil) your writing with bad gram**mar**.

guarantee
The **guar**d, **an** old friend, will **tee** off at three o'clock.

hangar
A han**gar** is like a **gar**age for planes.

hanger
Do you feel **anger** when your clothes fall off your h**anger**?

hear
With my **ear** I h**ear**.

here, there, where
All three words end with "**ere**."

immigrant
Many **m**illions of people were **grant**ed the right to be i**mmi**grants.

inoculation
An **in**oculation is when the doctor sticks the needle **in**.

interrupt
It's **r**eally **r**ude to inte**rr**upt someone.

it's
If you can substitute "**it is**," then it's "**it's.**"

language
This langu**age** has been spoken since a long-ago **age.**

library
It's **rar**e not to find a good book in the lib**rar**y.

license
Do **lice** have a **lice**nse to live here?

loose, noose, goose
Take the n**oose** off the neck of the l**oose** g**oose**.

lose
Did the clown l**ose** his rubber n**ose**?

maintenance
The **main** thing is for **ten** of the **mainten**ance men to fix the leak.

mantel
Can the **man tel**ephone from the **mantel**?

marriage
If I **marr**y, will **I age** faster after my **marriage**?

mathematics
Ma, the mat has **mathemat**ics written on it.

medieval
Did many people **die** in me**die**val times?

mileage
mile + **age** = **mileage**

miscellaneous
In his **cell**, the prisoner found mis**cell**aneous things.

misspell
Miss Pell would **misspell** everything!

naive
An**na**, **I've** been so **naive**.

niece
This p**iece** belongs to my n**iece**.

occasion
This special o**cca**sion calls for **c**oconut **c**ustard and **s**oda.

occur
When did the **c**ar **c**rash o**cc**ur?

often
She gives the right answer nine out **of ten** times, which is pretty **often**.

ough words
I'm t**ough** and thor**ough**, and I f**ough**t thr**ough** the r**ough** storm, and I th**ough**t I had s**ough**t and b**ough**t and br**ough**t enough c**ough** syrup for the whole winter.

pageant

page + ant = pageant

pajamas

Did **Pa jam** his **pajam**as in the drawer?

parallel

The two **l**'s in para**ll**el are parallel lines.

pavilion

There's a **lion** in the pavi**lion**!

peace

There's pe**ace** in this pl**ace**.

physician

What is the **ph**ysician's **ph**one number?

piece

Please cut me a **pie**ce of **pie**.

playwright

The play**wr**ight **wr**ote a beautiful play.

porpoise

Is that n**oise** coming from the porp**oise**?

potatoes

Her **toes** looked like little pota**toes**.

prairie

The **air** on the pr**air**ie is fresh and clean.

prey

Predators **pre**y on other animals.

principal

The princi**pal** of the school is your **pal**.

principle
A princi**ple** is a ru**le** of life.

professor
A pro**fess**or is **f**requently **s**omeone **s**mart.

pronunciation
The **nun** has clear pro**nun**ciation.

purchase
She opened her **pur**se to make her **pur**chase.

quiet
Try a qu**iet** d**iet**.

quite
You have qu**ite** an appet**ite**.

raspberry
G**rasp** the **rasp**berry and squeeze it.

realize
I **real**ized the diamond was **real**.

receipt
Shh! The **p** is silent in recei**p**t.

recipe
The rec**ipe** calls for **ripe** vegetables.

resistance
Sis has a **tan** in re**sis**tan**ce.

restaurant
Rest, dinos**aur** and **ant**, at this **restaurant**.

rhinoceros
The **rh**inoceros writes **rh**ymes.

ridiculous
He had to get **rid** of his **rid**iculous hat.

role
He has a **role** in the wh**ole** play.

roll
I tried to **roll** the tr**oll** over the kn**oll**.

safety
Be **safe**. Practice **safe**ty.

scene
I was **sc**ared by that **sc**ene in the movie.

scheme
He hatched a **sch**eme to get out of **sch**ool.

scissors
With **sc**issors, he cut the hair off his **sc**alp.

secretary
That **secret**ary has a **secret** she's not telling.
There's **tar** on the secre**tar**y's shoes.

separate
There's **a rat** in sep**arat**e.

shriek
"D**ie**!" he shr**ie**ked.

skiing
Keep both your *i*'s open when sk**ii**ng.

soldier
The sol**die**r did not **die**.

squeak
Does the mouse sp**eak** with a squ**eak**?

stationary
The **a** in station**a**ry stands for st**a**y.

stationery
The **e** in station**e**ry stands for **e**nvelope.

steal
Did he st**eal** the **real** treasure?

steel
The wh**eel** is made of st**eel**.

surgeon
I will **urge on** the s**urge on** to perform the operation.

sword
Take my **word** for it, this s**word** is sharp.

than
I like this pl**an** better th**an** Dan's pl**an**.

their, there, they're
All three begin with "**the**."

thief
A th**ief** will **lie**.

tomorrow
Tom, there will be no s**orrow tomorrow**.

tongue
An elephant's **tongue** weighs a **ton**, and he uses it to ar**gue**.

tragedy

Old **age** is not a trag**age**dy.

trouble

This is not **ou**r trou**ble**; it's y**our** trou**ble**.

vacuum

Make sure to vac**uu**m **up** **u**nder the sofa.

villain

The **villain** lives in a **villa in** the country.

weather

In rainy **weather**, **we** look **at her** picture.

Wednesday

She will **wed** next **Wed**nesday.

which

Wh**ich rich** person donated the money?

witch

The w**itch** scratched her **itch**.

yacht

This is the b**ach**elor's y**ach**t.

yolk

The gentle **folk** eat the y**olk**.

aard•vark

ab•a•cus

ab•a•lo•ne

a•ban•don

a•bate

a•bate•ment

a•bat•ing

ab•bey

ab•bot

ab•bre•vi•ate

ab•bre•vi•at•ing

ab•bre•vi•a•tion

ab•di•cate

ab•di•cat•ing

ab•di•ca•tion

ab•do•men

ab•dom•i•nal

ab•duct

ab•duc•tion

ab•duc•tor

ab•hor•rent

a•bide

a•bid•ing

a•bil•i•ties

a•bil•i•ty

a•blaze

a•ble

a•ble-bod•ied

a•bly

ab•nor•mal

ab•nor•mal•i•ty

a•board

a•bode

a•bol•ish

a•bo•li•tion

a•bo•li•tion•ist

a•bom•i•na•ble

a•bom•i•na•bly

ab•o•rig•i•nal

Ab•o•rig•i•ne

a•bound

a•bout

a•bove

a•bove•board

ab•ra•ca•dab•ra

a•brade

a•bra•sion

ab•ra•sive

a•breast

a•bridge

a•bridged

ablaze

a•bridg•ing

a•bridg•ment

a•broad

a•brupt

a•brupt•ly

ab•scess

ab•sence

ab•sent

ab•sent-mind•ed

ab•so•lute

ab•so•lute•ly

ab•so•lu•tion

ab•solve

ab•so•lu•tion

ab•sorb

ab•sorb•ent

ab•sorp•tion

ab•stain

ab•sten•tion

ab•sti•nence

ab•stract (adj. and n.)

ab•stract (v.)

ab•strac•tion

ab•surd

ab•sur•di•ties

ab•sur•di•ty

a•bun•dance

a•bun•dant

a•buse

a•bus•ing

a•bu•sive

a•byss

ac•a•**dem**•ic
ac•a•**dem**•i•cal•ly
a•**cad**•e•mies
a•**cad**•e•my
a cap•**pel**•la
ac•**cel**•er•ate
ac•**cel**•er•at•ing
ac•cel•er•**a**•tion
ac•**cel**•er•a•tor
ac•cent
ac•**cen**•tu•ate
ac•**cept** (sounds like "except")
I accept your kind offer.
ac•cept•a•**bil**•i•ty
ac•**cept**•a•ble
ac•**cept**•ance
ac•cess
ac•**ces**•si•ble
ac•**ces**•so•ry
ac•ci•dent
ac•ci•**den**•tal
ac•ci•**den**•tal•ly
ac•**claim**
ac•cla•**ma**•tion
ac•**com**•mo•date
ac•com•mo•**dat**•ing
ac•com•mo•**da**•tion
ac•**com**•pa•nied
ac•**com**•pa•nies
ac•**com**•pa•ni•ment
ac•**com**•pa•nist
ac•**com**•pa•ny

ac•**com**•plice
ac•**com**•plish
ac•**com**•plish•ment
ac•**cord**
ac•**cor**•dance
ac•**cor**•di•on
ac•**cor**•di•on•ist
ac•**cost**
ac•**count**
ac•count•a•**bil**•i•ty
ac•**count**•a•ble
ac•**count**•ant
ac•**cu**•mu•late
ac•**cu**•mu•lat•ing
ac•cu•mu•**la**•tion
ac•cu•ra•cy
ac•cu•rate
ac•cu•**sa**•tion
ac•**cuse**
ac•**cus**•ing
ac•**cus**•tomed
ace
ac•e•tate
ac•e•tone
a•**cet**•y•lene
ache
a•**chieve**
a•**chieve**•ment
a•**chiev**•ing
A•**chil**•les
ach•ing
ac•id
a•**cid**•ic
a•**cid**•i•ty

ac•**knowl**•edge
ac•**knowl**•edg•ing
ac•**knowl**•edg•ment
ac•ne
a•corn
a•**cou**•stic
a•**cou**•stics
ac•**quain**•tance
ac•**quire**
ac•**quir**•ing
ac•**quit**
ac•**quit**•tal
ac•**quit**•ted
a•cre
a•cre•age
ac•ro•bat
ac•ro•**bat**•ics
ac•ro•nym
a•**crop**•o•lis
a•**cross**
a•**cryl**•ic
act
act•ing
ac•tion
ac•ti•vate
ac•ti•vat•ing
ac•ti•**va**•tion
ac•ti•va•tor
ac•tive
ac•**tiv**•i•ty
ac•tor
ac•tress
ac•tu•al
ac•tu•**al**•i•ty

ac•tu•al•ly
ac•u•punc•ture
a•**cute**
ad
ad•age
a•**da**•gi•o
ad•a•mant
a•**dapt**
a•dapt•a•**bil**•i•ty
a•**dapt**•a•ble
ad•ap•**ta**•tion
a•**dapt**•er
(or a•**dap**•tor)
a•**dap**•tive
add

add

ad•dend
ad•**den**•dum
ad•dict
ad•**dic**•tion
ad•**dic**•tive
ad•**di**•tion
ad•**di**•tion•al

ad•di•tive
ad•**dress**
also pronounced
ad•dress
ad•dress•**ee**
ad•e•noid
ad•e•qua•cy
ad•e•quate
ad•**here**
ad•**he**•sion
ad•**he**•sive
a•**dieu**
a•di•**os**
ad•**ja**•cent
ad•jec•tive
ad•**journ**
ad•**journ**•ment
ad•**just**
ad•**just**•a•ble
ad•**just**•ment
ad lib
ad•**min**•is•ter
ad•**min**•is•tra•tor
ad•mi•ra•ble
ad•mi•ral
ad•**mire**
ad•**mir**•ing
ad•**mis**•si•ble
ad•**mis**•sion
ad•**mit**
ad•**mit**•tance
ad•**mit**•ted
ad•**mit**•ting
ad•**mon**•ish

ad•mo•**ni**•tion
a•**do**•be
ad•o•**les**•cence
ad•o•**les**•cent
a•**dopt**
a•**dop**•tion
a•**dor**•a•ble
ad•o•**ra**•tion
a•**dore**
a•**dor**•ing
a•**dorn**
a•**dorned**
a•**dorn**•ment
ad•**ren**•a•lin
a•**drift**
a•**dult**
also pronounced
a•dult
a•**dult**•hood
ad•**vance**
ad•**vanc**•ing
ad•**van**•tage
ad•van•**ta**•geous
ad•vent
ad•**ven**•ture
ad•**ven**•tur•er
ad•**ven**•ture•some
ad•**ven**•tur•ous
ad•verb
ad•ver•sar•ies
ad•ver•sar•y
ad•**verse**
ad•**ver**•si•ties
ad•**ver**•si•ty

ad•ver•tise
ad•ver•**tise**•ment
  also pronounced
  ad•**ver**•tise•ment
ad•**vice**
ad•vis•a•**bil**•i•ty
ad•**vis**•a•ble
ad•**vise**
ad•**vis**•er (*or* ad•**vis**•or)
ad•vo•cate (v.)
ad•vo•**cate** (n.)
ad•vo•cat•ing
aer•i•al
aer•i•al•ist
aer•o•**bat**•ics
aer•**o**•bics
aer•o•dy•**nam**•ic
aer•o•**nau**•ti•cal
aer•o•**nau**•tics
aer•o•sol
aer•o•space
Ae•sop
af•fa•ble
af•**fair**
af•**fect** (may sound like "effect")
  The weather may affect our plans.
af•**fect**•ed
af•**fec**•tion
af•**fec**•tion•ate
af•**fec**•tive
af•**fil**•i•ate
af•**fil**•i•at•ing

af•fil•i•**a**•tion
af•**firm**
af•fir•**ma**•tion
af•**firm**•a•tive
af•**flu**•ence
af•**flu**•ent
af•**ford**
af•**ford**•a•ble
af•ghan
a•**float**

afloat

a•**fraid**
a•**fresh**
Af•ri•can A•**mer**•i•can
Af•ro
aft
af•ter
af•ter•math
af•ter•**noon**
af•ter•thought
af•ter•ward (*or*

af•ter•wards)
a•**gain**
a•**gainst**
ag•ate
age
aged
  also pronounced
  a•ged
age•ism
age•less
a•gen•cy
a•**gen**•da
a•gent
ag•gra•vate
ag•gra•vat•ing
ag•gra•**va**•tion
ag•gre•gate
ag•**gres**•sion
ag•**gres**•sive
a•**ghast**
ag•ile
a•**gil**•i•ty
ag•ing
ag•i•tate
ag•i•tat•ing
ag•i•**ta**•tion
a•**go**
ag•o•nies
ag•o•nize
ag•o•ny
a•**gree**
a•**gree**•a•ble
a•**greed**
a•**gree**•ment

ag•ri•**cul**•tur•al
ag•ri•cul•ture
a•**ground**
a•**head**
a•**hoy**
aid (sounds like "aide")
  *They gave aid to
  the refugees.*
aide (sounds like "aid")
  *The aide works closely
  with the doctor.*
AIDS
ai•**ki**•do
ail•ment
aim
aim•less
air (sounds like "heir")
  Birds fly in the air.
air con•**di**•tion•er
air con•**di**•tion•ing
air•craft
air•craft **car**•ri•er
air•field
air force
air•line
air•mail
air•plane
air•port
air raid
air•ship
air•sick
air•sick•ness
air•strip
air•tight

air•wor•thy
air•y
aisle (sounds like "I'll"
  and "isle")
  *The bride walked
  down the aisle.*
a•**jar**
a•**kim**•bo
a•**kin**
Al•a•**bam**•a
a•la•bas•ter
a la **carte**
a la **mode**
a•**larm**
a•**las**
A•**las**•ka
al•ba•tross
al•**bi**•no
al•bum
al•che•mist
al•che•my
al•co•hol
al•co•**hol**•ic
al•co•**hol**•ism
al•cove
al•der
ale
a•**lert**
al•**fal**•fa
al•gae
al•ge•bra
al•ge•**bra**•ic
a•li•as
al•i•bi

al•ien
al•ien•**a**•tion
a•**lign**
a•**lign**•ment
a•**like**
al•i•**men**•ta•ry
  ca•**nal**
al•i•mo•ny
a•**live**
al•ka•li
al•ka•line
all (sounds like
  "awl")
  We ate all the food.
Al•lah
al•**lay**
al•le•**ga**•tion
al•**lege**
al•**leged**
al•**leg**•ed•ly
al•**le**•giance
al•le•**gor**•i•cal
al•le•go•ry
al•**ler**•gic
al•**le**•vi•ate
al•**le**•vi•at•ing
al•ley
al•**li**•ance
al•lied
  also pronounced
  al•**lied**
al•lies
al•li•ga•tor
al•lit•er•**a**•tion

al•**lot** (sounds like "a lot")

How much time did we allot for math?

al•**lot**•ment

al•**lot**•ted

al•**low**

al•**low**•a•ble

al•**low**•ance

al•**low**•ed

al•loy

all right

al•**lude** (sounds like "elude")

I allude to the president's speech where the idea was mentioned.

al•**lud**•ing

al•ly

al•ma **ma**•ter

al•ma•nac

al•**might**•y

al•mond

al•most

al•oe

a•**loft**

a•**lo**•ha

a•**lone**

a•**long**

a•long•**side**

a•**loof**

a•**loof**•ness

a lot (sounds like "allot")

She likes fudge a lot.

a•**loud**

al•**pac**•a

al•**pha**•bet

al•pha•**bet**•i•cal

al•**pha**•bet•ize

al•**read**•y

al•so

al•tar (sounds like "alter")

I prayed at the altar.

al•ter (sounds like "altar")

I'm going to alter my dress.

al•ter•**a**•tion

al•ter•**ca**•tion

al•ter **e**•go

al•ter•nate

al•ter•nat•ing

al•**ter**•na•tive

al•**though**

al•**tim**•e•ter

al•ti•tude

al•to

al•to•**geth**•er

al•tos

a•**lu**•mi•num

a•**lum**•na (f. sing.)

a•**lum**•nae (f. pl.)

a•**lum**•ni (m. pl.)

a•**lum**•nus (m. sing.)

al•ways

am

am•a•teur

am•a•**teur**•ish

a•**maze**

a•**maze**•ment

a•**maz**•ing

am•**bas**•sa•dor

am•ber

am•bi•dex•**ter**•i•ty

am•bi•**dex**•trous

am•bi•**gu**•i•ty

am•**big**•u•ous

am•**bi**•tion

am•**bi**•tious

am•**biv**•a•lence

am•**biv**•a•lent

am•ble

am•bling

am•bu•lance

ambulance

am•bu•la•to•ry

am•bush

a•**men**

a•**mend**

a•**mend**•ment
A•**mer**•i•ca
A•**mer**•i•can
A•**mer**•i•can **In**•di•an
am•e•thyst
a•mi•a•**bil**•i•ty
a•**mi**•a•ble
a•**mi**•a•bly
a•**mi**•go
Am•ish
am•**mo**•nia
am•mu•**ni**•tion
am•**ne**•sia
am•nes•ty
a•**moe**•ba (sing.)
a•**moe**•bae (pl.)
a•**moe**•bas (pl.)
a•**mong**
a•**mongst**
a•**mount**
amp
am•**phi**•bi•an
am•**phib**•i•ous
am•phi•the•a•ter
am•ple
am•pli•fi•**ca**•tion
am•pli•fied
am•pli•fi•er
am•pli•fies
am•pli•fy
am•pli•fy•ing
am•ply
am•pu•tate
am•pu•tat•ing

am•pu•**ta**•tion
am•pu•**tee**
a•**muse**
a•**muse**•ment
a•**mus**•ing
an
an•a•**con**•da
an•a•gram
an•a•log
a•**nal**•y•ses
a•**nal**•y•sis
an•a•lyze
an•a•lyz•ing
an•a•**tom**•i•cal
a•**nat**•o•my
an•ces•tor
an•ces•try
an•chor
an•cho•vies
an•cho•vy
  also pronounced
  an•**cho**•vy
an•cient
and
an•droid
an•ec•dote
a•**ne**•mi•a
a•**ne**•mic
a•**nem**•o•ne
an•es•**the**•sia
an•es•**thet**•ic
a•**nes**•the•tist
a•**nes**•the•tize
a•**new**

an•gel (often confused
  with "angle")
  An angel has wings.
an•ger
an•gle (often confused
  with "angel")
  This triangle has a
  right angle.
an•**go**•ra
an•gri•ly
an•gry
an•guish
an•gu•lar
an•i•mal
an•i•mat•ed
an•i•mat•ing
an•i•**ma**•tion
an•i•**mos**•i•ty
an•kle
an•nex
  also pronounced
  an•**nex**
an•**ni**•hi•late
an•ni•hi•**la**•tion
an•**ni**•hi•la•tor
an•ni•**ver**•sa•ries
an•ni•**ver**•sa•ry
an•no•tate
an•no•**ta**•tion
an•**nounce**
an•**nounce**•ment
an•**nounc**•er
an•**nounc**•ing
an•**noy**

an•**noy**•ance
an•nu•al
an•**nul**
an•**nulled**
an•**nul**•ling
an•**nul**•ment
a•**noint**
an•o•**nym**•i•ty
a•**non**•y•mous
an•o•**rak**
an•o•**rex**•ic
an•**oth**•er
an•swer
an•swer•a•ble
ant (sounds like "aunt")

An ant crawled into our picnic.

an•**tag**•o•nism
an•**tag**•o•nist
an•tag•o•**nis**•tic
an•**tag**•o•nize
an•**tag**•o•niz•ing
Ant•**arc**•tic
Ant•**arc**•ti•ca
ant•eat•er
an•te•**ced**•ent
an•te•lope
an•**ten**•na
an•them
an•ther
an•**thol**•o•gy
an•thra•cite
an•thro•**pol**•o•gist

an•thro•**pol**•o•gy
an•ti•bi•**ot**•ic
an•ti•bod•y
an•**tic**•i•pate
an•**tic**•i•pat•ing
an•**tic**•i•pa•tion
an•ti•**cli**•max
an•ti•dote
an•ti•freeze
an•ti•**his**•ta•mine
an•ti•**pas**•to
an•ti•**per**•spi•rant
an•**tique**
an•ti•**Sem**•i•tism
an•ti•**sep**•tic
an•ti•**so**•cial
an•ti•**tox**•in
an•ti•**trust**
ant•ler
an•to•nym
anx•**i**•e•ty
anx•ious
an•y
an•y•bod•y
an•y•how
an•y•**more**
an•y•one
an•y•place
an•y•thing
an•y•time
an•y•way
an•y•where
a•**or**•ta
A•**pach**•e

a•**part**
a•**part**•heid
a•**part**•ment
ap•a•**thet**•ic
ap•a•thy
ape
ap•er•ture
a•pex
a•**piece**
a•pol•o•**get**•ic
a•**pol**•o•gies
a•**pol**•o•gize
a•**pol**•o•giz•ing
a•**pol**•o•gy
a•**pos**•tle
a•**pos**•tro•phe
ap•**pall**•ing
ap•pa•**rat**•us
ap•**par**•el
ap•**par**•ent
ap•pa•**ri**•tion
ap•**peal**
ap•**peal**•ing
ap•**pear**
ap•**pear**•ance
ap•**pease**
ap•**pen**•di•ces
ap•pen•di•**ci**•tis
ap•**pen**•dix
ap•**pen**•dix•es
ap•pe•tite
ap•pe•tiz•er
ap•pe•tiz•ing
ap•**plaud**

ap•**plaud**•ed
ap•**plause**
ap•ple
ap•ple•sauce
ap•**pli**•ance
ap•pli•cant
ap•pli•**ca**•tion
ap•**ply**
ap•**point**
ap•**point**•ment
ap•po•**si**•tion
ap•**prais**•al
ap•**praise**
ap•**pre**•ci•ate
ap•**pre**•ci•at•ing
ap•**pre**•ci•a•tive
ap•pre•**hend**
ap•pre•**hen**•sive
ap•**pren**•tice
ap•**pren**•tice•ship
ap•**proach**
ap•**proach**•a•ble
ap•**pro**•pri•ate
ap•**prove**
ap•**prov**•ing
ap•**prox**•i•mate
ap•prox•i•**ma**•tion
a•pri•cot
A•pril
a•pron
apt
ap•ti•tude
Aq•ua-Lung
aq•ua•ma•**rine**

a•**quar**•i•um
a•**quat**•ic
aq•ue•duct
A•**ra**•bi•a
Ar•a•bic
ar•a•ble
ar•bi•trar•y
ar•bi•trate
ar•bi•**trat**•ing
ar•bi•**tra**•tion
ar•bi•tra•tor
ar•bor
arc
ar•**cade**
arch
ar•chae•**o**•lo•gy (*or*
  ar•che•**ol**•o•gy)
ar•che•**ol**•o•gist
ar•che•o•**log**•i•cal
ar•**cha**•ic
arch•**bish**•op
arch•duke

Aqua-Lung

arch•e•ry
ar•chi•**pel**•a•go
ar•chi•tect
ar•chi•**tec**•tur•al
ar•chi•tec•ture
ar•chives
arch•way
arc•tic
Arc•tic **Cir**•cle
ar•dent
ar•dor
ar•du•ous
are
ar•e•a
a•**re**•na
aren't
Ar•gen•**ti**•na
ar•gue
ar•gu•ing
ar•gu•ment
ar•gu•**men**•ta•tive
a•ria
ar•id
a•**rise**
a•**ris**•en
a•**ris**•ing
ar•is•**toc**•ra•cy
a•**ris**•to•crat
a•ris•to•**crat**•ic
Ar•is•tot•le
a•**rith**•me•tic
Ar•i•**zo**•na
Ar•kan•sas
ark

arm
ar•**ma**•da
ar•ma•**dil**•lo
ar•ma•**dil**•los
arm•chair
Ar•**me**•ni•a
arm•ful
ar•mies
ar•mis•tice
ar•mor
ar•mor•ies
ar•mor•y
arm•pit
ar•my
a•**ro**•ma
a•ro•**mat**•ic
a•**round**
a•**rouse**
a•**rous**•ing
ar•**raign**
ar•**range**
ar•**ranged**
ar•**range**•ment
ar•**rang**•ing
ar•**rest**
ar•**ri**•val
ar•**rive**
ar•ro•gant
ar•row
ar•row•head
ar•se•nal
ar•se•nic
ar•son
art

ar•ter•ies
ar•te•ri•o•scle•**ro**•sis
ar•ter•y
ar•**thrit**•ic
ar•**thri**•tis
ar•thro•pod
ar•ti•choke
ar•tic•le
ar•**tic**•u•late
ar•**tic**•u•lat•ing
ar•ti•fact
ar•ti•**fi**•cial
ar•**til**•ler•y
ar•ti•san
art•ist
ar•**tis**•tic
art•ist•ry
as
as•**bes**•tos
as•**cend**
ash
a•**shamed**
ash•en
a•**shore**
A•sia
A•sian A•**mer**•i•can
a•**side**
ask
a•**skew**
a•**sleep**
as•**par**•a•gus
as•pect
as•pen
as•phalt

as•**phyx**•i•ate
as•**phyx**•i•at•ing
as•phyx•i•**a**•tion
as•pi•**ra**•tion
as•pi•rin
as•**sas**•sin
as•**sas**•si•nate
as•**sas**•si•nat•ing
as•**sas**•si•na•tion
as•**sault**
as•**sem**•ble
as•**sem**•blies
as•**sem**•bling
as•**sem**•bly
as•**sent**
as•**sert**
as•**ser**•tion
as•**ser**•tive
as•**sess**
as•**sess**•ment
as•**ses**•sor
as•set
as•**sign**
as•**sign**•ing
as•**sign**•ment
as•**sist**
as•**sist**•ance (sounds like "assistants")
I need your assistance to move this desk.
as•**sist**•ant
as•**sist**•ants (sounds like "assistance")
She has four assistants.

as•**so**•ci•ate
as•**so**•ci•at•ing
as•so•ci•**a**•tion
as•**sort**•ment
as•**sume**
as•**sum**•ing
as•**sump**•tion
as•**sur**•ance
as•**sure**
as•**sur**•ing
as•ter
as•ter•isk
as•ter•oid

asteroid

asth•ma
asth•**mat**•ic
a•**stig**•ma•tism
as•**ton**•ish
as•**ton**•ish•ment
as•**tound**
as•**tound**•ing
a•**stray**

a•**stride**
as•**trin**•gent
as•tro•dome
as•**trol**•o•ger
as•tro•**log**•i•cal
as•**trol**•o•gy
as•tro•naut
as•**tron**•o•mer
as•tro•**nom**•i•cal
as•**tron**•o•my
as•tro•**phys**•ics
as•**tute**
a•**sy**•lum
a•sym•**met**•ric
a•sym•**met**•ri•cal
a•**sym**•me•try
at
ate (sounds like"eight")
    I ate the whole cake
    myself.
a•the•ism
a•the•ist
Ath•ens
ath•lete
ath•**let**•ic
ath•**let**•i•cal•ly
ath•**let**•ics
At•**lan**•tic
at•las
at•mos•phere
at•mos•**pher**•ic
at•oll
at•om
a•**tom**•ic

a•**tone**
a•tri•um
a•**tro**•cious
a•**troc**•i•ty
at•**tach**
at•ta•**ché**
at•**tack**
at•**tain**
at•**tain**•ment
at•**tempt**
at•**tend**
at•**ten**•dance
at•**ten**•dant
at•**ten**•tion
at•**ten**•tive
at•**test**
at•tic
at•**tire**
at•ti•tude
at•**tor**•ney
at•**tract**
at•**trac**•tion
at•**trac**•tive
at•**trib**•ute (n.)
at•**trib**•ute (v.)
au•burn
auc•tion
auc•tion•**eer**
au•di•ble
au•di•bly
au•di•ence
au•di•o
au•di•o•tape
au•di•o•**vis**•u•al

au•**di**•tion

au•di•**to**•ri•um

au•**di**•to•ry

Au•du•bon

Au•gust

auld lang **syne**

aunt (sounds like "ant")

My aunt gave me a book.

au pair

au•ral (sounds like "oral")

Aural information comes in through your ear.

au•ri•cle

au•**ro**•ra bo•re•**al**•is

aus•**tere**

aus•**ter**•i•ty

au•**then**•tic

au•thor

au•thor•i•**tar**•i•an

au•**thor**•i•ta•tive

au•**thor**•i•ty

au•thor•i•**za**•tion

au•thor•ize

au•thor•iz•ing

au•thor•ship

au•**tis**•tic

au•to•bi•**og**•ra•pher

au•to•bi•o•**graph**•i•cal

au•to•bi•**og**•ra•phy

au•to•graph

au•to•**mat**•ic

au•to•**mat**•i•cal•ly

au•to•**ma**•tion

au•**tom**•a•ton

au•to•mo•bile

au•to•**mo**•tive

au•**ton**•o•mous

au•**ton**•o•my

au•top•sy

au•tumn

aux•**il**•ia•ry

a•vail•a•**bil**•i•ty

a•**vail**•a•ble

av•a•lanche

a•vant **garde**

a•**venge**

a•**veng**•ing

av•e•nue

av•er•age

a•**vert**

a•vi•ar•y

a•vi•**a**•tion

av•id

av•o•**ca**•do

av•o•**ca**•tion

a•**void**

a•**void**•ance

a•**vow**

a•**wait**

a•**wake**

a•**wak**•en

a•**ward**

a•**ware**

a•**ware**•ness

a•**way** (sounds like "aweigh")

She went away yesterday.

awe

a•**weigh** (sounds like "away")

Anchors aweigh!

awe•some

aw•ful

aw•ful•ly

awk•ward

awl (sounds like "all")

With an awl he made holes in the leather.

aw•ning

a•**wry**

ax (*or* **axe**)

ax•is

ax•le

aye

a•**za**•lea

Az•tec

az•ure

bab•ble
bab•bling
bab•ied
ba•bies
ba•**boon**
ba•**bush**•ka
ba•by
ba•by•hood
ba•by•ish
Bab•y•lon
ba•by-**sit**•ter
ba•by-**sit**•ting
bach•e•lor
bach•e•lor•hood
back
back•board
back•bone
back•**door**
back•drop
back•er
back•field
back•fire
back•gam•mon
back•ground
back•hand
back•hoe
back•lash
back•log
back•pack
back•side
back•slide
back•stage

back•stroke
back talk
back•ward
back•wa•ter
back•yard

bagpipes

ba•con
bac•**te**•ri•a
bac•**te**•ri•al
bac•te•ri•o•**log**•i•cal
bac•te•ri•**ol**•o•gist
bac•te•ri•**ol**•o•gy
bad
badge
badg•er
bad•ly
bad•min•ton
bad•mouth

baf•fle
bag
ba•gel
bag•gage
bagged
bag•ging
bag•gy
bag•pip•er
bag•pipes
bail (sounds like "bale")
   She paid his bail.
bail•iff
bail out
bait
bake
bak•er•y
bak•ing
bak•ing **pow**•der
bak•ing **so**•da
bal•ance
bal•anc•ing
bal•co•nies
bal•con•y
bald
bald•ness
bale (sounds like "bail")
   *A bale of hay fell
   on him.*
Bal•kan
ball (sounds like
   "bawl")
   Throw the ball gently.

bal•lad
bal•last
ball **bear**•ings
bal•le•**ri**•na
bal•let
bal•**lis**•tics
bal•loon
bal•lot
ball•play•er
ball•point
ball•room
balm•i•ness
balm•y
bal•sa
bal•sam
Bal•tic
Bal•ti•more
bam•**boo**
bam•**boo**•zle
ban
ba•**nan**•a
band
band•age
band•ag•ing
ban•**dan**•na
ban•dit
band•mas•ter
band•wag•on
bang
ban•gle
bangs
ban•ish
ban•ish•ment
ban•is•ter

ban•jo
ban•jos (*or*
  ban•joes)
bank
bank•er
bank•ing
bank•rupt
bank•rupt•cy
banned
ban•ner
ban•ning
ban•quet
ban•tam
ban•ter
bap•**tize**
bap•**tiz**•ing
bar
bar•**bar**•i•an

bandage

bar•**bar**•i•an•ism
bar•**bar**•ic
bar•be•cue
bar•be•cu•ing

barbed wire
bar•ber
bar•ber•shop
Bar•ce•**lo**•na
bar code
bare (sounds like
  "bear")
  *It's too cold to run
  around bare.*
bare•back
bare•faced
bare•foot
bare•**head**•ed
bare•ly
bar•gain
barge
barg•ing
bar graph
bar•i•tone
bar•i•um
bark
bar•ley
bar mitz•vah
barn
bar•na•cle
barn•storm•ing
barn•yard
ba•**rom**•e•ter
bar•o•**met**•ric
bar•on (sounds like
  "barren")
  *The baron lives in a
  palace.*
bar•on•ess

ba•**roque**

bar•racks

bar•ra•**cu**•da

bar•rel

bar•ren (sounds like "baron")

No crops grew on the barren fields.

bar•**rette**

bar•ri•cade

bar•ri•cad•ed

bar•ri•er

bar•ri•o

bar•ris•ter

bar•ten•der

bar•ter

base (sounds like "bass")

She slid into third base.

base•ball

base•board

base•less

base•ment

bas•es (sounds like "basis")

Cover all your bases.

bash

bash•ful

ba•sic

ba•si•cal•ly

ba•sin

ba•sis (sounds like "bases")

This is the basis of our idea.

bask

bas•ket

bas•ket•ball

bas mitz•vah

bass (sounds like "base")

He has a bass voice.

(rhymes with "class")

We fished for bass.

bass drum

bas•**soon**

baste

bat

batch

bath (n.)

bathe (v.)

bath•ing suit

bath•robe

bath•room

bath•tub

ba•**tik**

bat mitz•vah

ba•**ton**

bat•**tal**•ion

bat•ter

bat•ter•ing **ram**

bat•ter•y

bat•tle

bat•tle•field

bat•tle•ground

bat•tle•ship

bau•ble

bawd•y

bawl (sounds like "ball")

He'll bawl like a baby.

bay

bay•o•net

bay•ou

ba•**zaar** (sounds like "bizarre")

I bought this at the bazaar.

be

beach (sounds like "beech")

This beach is rocky.

bea•con

bead

bea•gle

beak

beak•er

beam

bean

bean•stalk

bear (sounds like "bare")

The grizzly bear growled loudly.

beard

bear•ing

bear•skin

beast

beat (sounds like "beet")

He likes to beat his drum.

beau•**ti**•cian
beau•ti•ful
beau•ty
bea•ver
be•**cause**
beck•on
be•**come**
be•**com**•ing
bed
be•**daz**•zle
be•**daz**•zling
bed•bug
bed•clothes
bed•ding
bed•fel•low
bed•lam
bed•ou•in
be•**drag**•gle
be•**drag**•gled
bed•rid•den
bed•rock
bed•room
bed•side
bed•spread
bed•time
bee
beech (sounds like "beach")

She climbed the beech tree.

beef
beef•steak
bee•hive
bee•line

been
beep
beer (sounds like "bier")

We don't serve beer to minors.

beet (sounds like "beat")

He makes delicious beet soup.

Bee•tho•ven
bee•tle
be•**fit**•ting
be•**fore**
be•**fore**•hand
be•**friend**
beg
be•**gan**
beg•gar
beg•ging
be•**gin**
be•**gin**•ner
be•**gin**•ning
be•**go**•ni•a
be•**grudge**
be•**guile**
be•**guil**•ing
be•**half**
be•**have**
be•**hav**•ior
be•**head**
be•**held**
be•**he**•moth
be•**hind**

be•**hold**
be•**hoove**
beige
be•ing
Bei•rut
be•**la**•bor
be•**lat**•ed
belch
bel•fry
Bel•gian (adj.)
Bel•gium (n.)
be•**lief**
be•**liev**•a•ble
be•**lieve**
be•**liev**•ing
be•**lit**•tle
be•**lit**•tling
bell
bell•boy
bell•hop
bel•li•cose
bel•lies
bel•**lig**•er•ence
bel•**lig**•er•ent
bel•low
bel•lows
bel•ly
bel•ly **but**•ton
be•**long**
be•**lov**•ed
be•**low**
belt
bench
bend

be•**neath**
ben•e•fac•tor
ben•e•**fi**•cial
ben•e•fit
ben•e•fit•ed
ben•e•fit•ing
be•**nev**•o•lence
be•**nev**•o•lent
be•**nign**
be•**queath**
be•**rate**
be•**rat**•ing
be•**reaved**
be•**reave**•ment
be•**ret**
ber•ries
ber•ry (sounds like "bury")

What kind of berry grows on this tree?

ber•**serk**
berth (sounds like "birth")

He slept in the upper berth on the train.

be•**seech**
be•**side**
be•**sides**
be•**siege**
best
be•**stow**
bet
Beth•le•hem
be•**tray**

be•**tray**•al
be•**tray**•er
bet•ter
bet•ting
be•**tween**
bev•er•age
be•**ware**
be•**wil**•der
be•**wil**•der•ment
be•**witch**
be•**yond**
bi•as
bi•ased
bi•**ath**•lon
Bi•ble
bib•li•cal
bib•li•**og**•ra•phy
bi•**cam**•er•al
bi•**car**•bo•nate
bi•cen•**ten**•ni•al
bi•ceps

(biceps)

bick•er
bi•**coast**•al
bi•**cus**•pid
bi•cy•cle
bi•cy•clist
bid
bid•der
bid•ding
bide
bier (sounds like "beer")

The corpse was placed on the funeral bier.

bi•fo•cals
big
big•ger
big•horn
big•ot
big•ot•ed
big•ot•ry
bike
bi•**ki**•ni
bile
bi•**lin**•gual
bill
bill•board
bill•fold
bil•liards
bil•lion
bil•lion•aire
bil•low
bil•low•y
bin
bi•na•ry

B

bind
bind·er
binge
bin·go
bin·oc·u·lars
bi·o·de·**grad**·a·ble
bi·o·di·**ver**·si·ty
bi·**og**·ra·pher
bi·o·**graph**·i·cal
bi·**og**·ra·phy
bi·**ol**·o·gy
bi·**on**·ic
bi·o·rhythm
bi·plane
birch
bird
birth (sounds like "berth")
We all celebrated the birth of the baby.
birth·day
birth·mark
birth·place
birth·rate
birth·right
birth·stone
bis·cuit
bi·sect
bi·**sec**·tion
bish·op
bi·son
bit
bite (sounds like "byte")

He took a big bite of cake.
bit·ing
bit·ter
bi·**zarre** (sounds like "bazaar")
Her outfit is bizarre.
blab
blabbed
blab·ber
blab·bing
blab·ber·mouth

blabbermouth

black
black·ball
black·ber·ry
black·bird
black·board
black·en
black eye
Black·foot
black hole
black·jack

black·mail
black·out
black·smith
black·top
blad·der
blade
blame
blame·less
bland
blank
blan·ket
blare
blar·ing
blas·phe·my
blast
blast·off
bla·tant
blaze
blaz·er
blaz·ing
bleach
bleach·ers
bleak
blear·y
bleed
blem·ish
blend
blend·er
bless
bless·ed
blew (sounds like "blue")
The bugler blew the horn.

blight
blimp
blind
blind•er
blind•fold
blind•ness
blink
bliss
bliss•ful
blis•ter
bliz•zard
bloat
bloat•ed
blob
bloc (sounds like "block")
The bloc of nations voted for peace.
block (sounds like "bloc")
Here's a block of wood to play with.
block•**ade**
block•**ad**•ing
blond
blood
blood•hound
blood•shed
blood•shot
blood•stream
blood•thirst•y
blood **ves**•sel
blood•y
bloom

bloom•ers
blos•som
blot
blotch
blotch•y
blot•ter
blot•ting
blouse
blow
blow•er
blow•torch
blow•up
blub•ber
bludg•eon
blue (sounds like "blew")
I wore my blue shirt.
Blue•beard
blue•ber•ry
blue•ber•ries
blue•bird
blue•fish
blue•grass
blue jay
blue jeans
blue•print
blues
blue whale
bluff
blun•der
blunt
blur
blurb
blurred

blur•ring
blur•ry
blurt
blush
blus•ter
blus•ter•y
bo•a con•**stric**•tor
boar (sounds like "bore")
The wild boar ran into the woods.
board
board•er
board•ing
boast
boast•ful
boat
boat•house
boat•ing
bob
bobbed
bob•bin
bob•bing
bob•by **pin**
bob•cat
bob•sled
bob•tail
bob•white
bode
bod•ing
bod•y
bod•y•guard
bog
bogged

bog•gy
bo•gus
boil
boil•er
boil•ing **point**
bois•ter•ous
bold
bold•face
boll wee•vil
bol•ster
bolt
bomb
bom•**bard**
bom•**bard**•ment
bom•**bas**•tic
Bom•**bay**
bomb•er
bomb•proof
bomb•shell
bo•na fide
bo•**nan**•za
Bo•na•parte
bon•bon
bond
bond•age
bone
bone-dry
bon•fire
bon•go **drum**
bon•net
bon•sai
    also pronounced
    bon•**sai**
bo•nus

bon voy•**age**
bon•y
boo•by **trap**
boog•ie-**woog**•ie
book
book•case
book club
book•end
book•keep•er
book•keep•ing
book•let
book•mark
book•mo•bile
book•store
book•worm
boom
boo•mer•ang
boon
boost
boos•ter
boot
booth
boot•leg
boo•ty
booze
bor•der
bore (sounds like
    "boar")
*I hope my story
didn't bore you.*
bore•dom
bor•ing
born (sounds like
    "borne")

*My brother was born
on a Tuesday.*
borne (sounds like
    "born")
*The donkey has borne
a heavy load.*
bor•ough (sounds like
    "burro" and "burrow")
*He lives in another
borough of the city.*
bor•row
bos•om
boss
boss•y
Bos•ton
bo•**tan**•i•cal
bot•a•nist
bot•a•ny
both
both•er
both•er•some
bot•tle
bot•tle•neck
bot•tling
bot•tom
bough (rhymes with
    "wow")
*She climbed out onto
the bough of the tree.*
bought
bouil•lon (sounds like
    "bullion")
*Drink this clear
chicken bouillon.*
boul•der

bou•le•vard
bounce
bounc•ing
bound
bound•a•ries
bound•a•ry
bound•less
boun•ti•ful
boun•ty
bou•**quet**
bour•bon
bout
bou•**tique**
bo•vine
bow (rhymes with "go")

She tied a bow in her hair.

bow (rhymes with "cow")

Take a bow after your performance.

bow•els
bowl
bow•leg•ged
bowl•ing
box
box•car
box•er
box•es
boy
boy•cott
boy•friend
boy•hood

bra
brace
brace•let
brac•ing
brack•et
brag
bragged
Brah•ma
braid

braid

Braille
brain
brain•child
brain•storm
brain•wash
brain•y
brake (sounds like "break")

Step on the brake to stop the car.

brake•man
brak•ing
bram•ble
bran
branch

branch•es
brand
bran•dish
brand-new
brand•y
brass
brass•y
brat
bra•**va**•do
brave
brav•er•y
bra•vo
brawl
brawn•i•er
bra•zen
Bra•**zil**
breach
bread
breadth
bread•win•ner
break (sounds like "brake")

I didn't break it.

break•down
break•er
break•fast
break-in
break•neck
break•through
break•wa•ter
breast
breast•bone
breast•plate
breast•stroke

breath (n.)
breathe (v.)
breath•er
breath•ing
breath•less
breath•tak•ing
breech•es
breed
breeze
breez•i•ly
breez•y
brev•i•ty
brew
brew•er•y
bri•ar
bribe
brib•ing
brick
brick•lay•er
brick•work
brid•al (sounds like "bridle")

The bridal party has two bridesmaids.

bride
bride•groom
brides•maid
bridge
bri•dle (sounds like "bridal")

Ride the horse on the bridle path.

brief
brief•case

bri•er
brig
bri•**gade**
bright
bright•en
bril•liance
bril•liant
brim
brim•ful

bricklayer

brim•med
brim•ming
brine
bring
brink
brisk
bris•tle
bris•tling
Brit•ain

Brit•ish
brit•tle
broach (sounds like "brooch")

He hated to broach the subject.

broad
broad•cast
broad•en
broad-mind•ed
broad•side
bro•**cade**
broc•co•li
bro•**chure**
broil•er
broke
bro•ken
bro•ken•**heart**•ed
bro•ker
bro•ker•age
bron•chi•al
bron•**chi**•tis
bron•co
bron•to•saur•us
bronze
Bronze Age
brooch (sounds like "broach")

She wore a diamond brooch.

brood
brook
Brook•lyn
broom

broom·stick
broth
broth·er
broth·er·hood
broth·er-in-law
broth·ers-in-law
brought
brow
brow·beat
brown
brown·ie
brown·out
brown·stone
browse
brows·ing
bruise
bruis·ing
brunch
bru·**nette**
brunt
brush
brusque
Brus·sels sprout
bru·tal
bru·**tal**·i·ty
brute
bub·ble
bub·bling
bub·bly
bu·**bon**·ic
buc·ca·**neer**
buck
buck·a·roo
buck·board

buck·et
buck·le
buck·ling
buck·shot
buck·skin
buck·tooth
buck·wheat
bud
Bud·dha
Bud·dhism
Bud·dhist
bud·ding
bud·dy
budge
budg·et
budg·ing
Bue·nos **Ai**·res
buff
buf·fa·lo
buff·er
buf·fet
buf·**foon**
bug
bugged
bug·ging
bug·gy
bu·gle
bu·gler
build
build·ing
built
built-in
bulb
bulge

bulg·ing
bulk
bulk·i·er
bulk·i·est
bulk·y
bull
bull·dog
bull·doz·er
bul·let
bul·le·tin
bul·let·proof
bull·fight
bull·frog
bul·lion (sounds like "bouillon")
There is gold bullion in the bank.
bull's-eye
bul·ly
bum·ble·bee
bum·bling
bump
bump·er
bump·i·er
bump·i·est
bump·y
bun
bunch
bun·dle
bun·dling
bun·ga·low
bun·gee cord
bun·gle
bunk

bun•ker
bunk•house
bun•ny
Bun•sen burn•er
bunt
bunt•ing
buoy
buoy•ant
bur (or burr)
bur•den
bur•den•some
bu•reau
bu•reauc•ra•cy
bu•reau•crat•ic
bur•ger
bur•glar
bur•glar•ize
bur•glar•proof
bur•glar•y
bur•i•al
bur•ied
bur•ies
bur•lap
bur•lesque
bur•li•ness
bur•ly
Bur•ma
Bur•mese
burn
burn•er
bur•nish
burnt
burp

bur•ri•to
bur•ro (sounds like
    "borough" and
    "burrow")
*She rode a little burro
into town.*
bur•row (sounds like
    "borough" and
    "burro")
*The rabbit tried to
burrow in the yard.*
burst
bur•y (sounds like
    "berry")
*Let's bury the
treasure.*
bur•y•ing
bus
bush
bush•el
bush•man
bush•whack
bush•y
bus•i•er
bus•i•est
busi•ness
busi•ness•like
bust
bus•tle
bus•tling
bus•y
bus•y•bod•y
but
butch•er

but•ler
but•ter
but•ter•cup
but•ter•fin•gers
but•ter•flies
but•ter•fly
but•ter•milk
but•ter•scotch
but•ter•y
but•ton
but•ton•hole
but•tress
buy (sounds like
    "by")
*How many pears did
you buy?*
buzz
buz•zard
buzz•er
by (sounds like "buy")
*This book is by
Mark Twain.*
by•gone
by•law
by•pass
by-prod•uct
by•stand•er
byte (sounds like
    "bite")
*A byte is a unit of
computer memory.*
by•word
Byz•an•tine

cab
cab•bage
cab•in
cab•i•net
ca•ble
ca•boose
ca•ca•o
cack•le
ca•coph•o•ny
cac•tus
ca•det
Cae•sar
ca•fé
caf•e•te•ri•a
caf•feine
  also pronounced
  caf•feine
caf•tan
cage
ca•gey
Cai•ro
ca•jole
Ca•jun
cake
ca•lam•i•ty
cal•ci•um
cal•cu•late
cal•cu•lat•ing
cal•cu•la•tor
cal•en•dar
calf
cal•i•co

Cal•i•for•nia
call
cal•lig•ra•pher
cal•lig•ra•phy
call•ing
cal•lous
cal•low
calm
cal•o•rie
calves
ca•lyp•so
cam•cord•er
came
cam•el
Cam•e•lot
cam•e•o

camera

cam•er•a
cam•er•a•per•son
cam•ou•flage
camp
cam•paign

cam•per
camp•fire
cam•phor
camp•us
can
Can•a•da
Ca•na•di•an
ca•nal
ca•nar•y
can•cel
can•celed
can•cel•ing
can•cel•la•tion
can•cer
can•cer•ous
can•de•la•bra
can•did
can•di•da•cy
can•di•date
can•died
can•dle
can•dle•light
can•dy
cane
ca•nine
canned
can•ner•y
can•ni•bal
can•non (sounds like
  "canon")
*The rebels fired the
cannon.*

can•ny
ca•**noe**
ca•**noe**•ing
can•on (sounds like
  "cannon")
  *The priest knew
  church canon.*
can•o•py
can't
can•ta•loupe
can•**tan**•ker•ous
can•**ta**•ta
can•**teen**
can•ter (sounds like
  "cantor")
  *This horse loves to
  canter.*
Can•ton•**ese**
can•tor (sounds
  like "canter")
  *The cantor sings
  in the synagogue.*
can•vas (sounds like
  "canvass")
  *The tent is made
  of canvas.*
can•vass (sounds like
  "canvas")
  *Canvass the people
  for their votes.*
can•yon
cap
ca•pa•**bil**•i•ties
ca•pa•**bil**•i•ty
ca•pa•ble

ca•**pac**•i•ty
cape
ca•per
cap•ful
cap•il•lar•y
cap•i•tal (sounds like
  "capitol")
  *Begin each sentence
  with a capital letter.*
cap•i•tal•ism
cap•i•tal•ist
cap•i•tol (sounds like
  "capital")
  *The legislature meets
  in the capitol building.*
cap•puc•**ci**•no
ca•**pri**•cious

(**capsize**)

cap•size
cap•**siz**•ing
cap•sule
cap•tain
cap•tion

cap•ti•vate
cap•ti•vat•ing
cap•tive
cap•**tiv**•i•ty
cap•tor
cap•ture
cap•tur•ing
car
car•a•mel
car•at (sounds like
  "karat," "caret," and
  "carrot")
  *This ring has a one-
  carat diamond.*
car•a•van
car•bide
car•bine
car•bo•**hy**•drates
car•bon
car•bu•re•tor
car•cass
card
card•board
car•di•ac
car•di•gan
car•di•nal
care
ca•**reer**
care•free
care•ful
care•giv•er
care•less
car•**ess**
car•et (sounds like

"carat," "carrot," and "karat")

The caret shows where to insert the word.

care•tak•er

car•fare

car•go

Ca•**rib**•be•an

car•i•bou

car•i•ca•ture

car•i•ca•tur•ist

car•jack

car•load

car•**na**•tion

car•ni•val

car•ni•vore

car•**niv**•o•rous

car•ob

car•ol

car•ol•er

Car•o•**li**•na

ca•**rouse**

ca•**rous**•ing

carp

car•pen•ter

car•pet

car•pet•bag•ger

car•pet•ing

car•pool (v.)

car pool (n.)

car•riage

car•ried

car•ri•er

car•ries

car•rot (sounds like "carat," "caret," and "karat")

Did you slice a carrot into the salad?

car•ry

car•ry•ing

car•sick

cart

carte blanche

car•ti•lage

car•**tog**•ra•pher

car•**tog**•ra•phy

car•ton

car•**toon**

car•**toon**•ist

car•tridge

cart•wheel

carve

carv•ing

cas•**cade**

cas•**cad**•ing

case

case•ment

cash

cash•ew

ca•**shier**

cash•mere

ca•**si**•no

cask

cas•ket

cas•se•role

cas•**sette**

cast (sounds like "caste")

She had a cast on her broken leg.

cast•a•way

caste (sounds like "cast")

She belongs to a high caste in that society.

cast iron

cas•tle

cas•u•al

cas•u•al•ty

cat

cat•a•comb

cat•a•log (or **cat**•a•logue)

cat•a•lyst

cat•a•ma•**ran**

cat•a•pult

cat•a•ract

ca•**tas**•tro•phe

ca•ta•**stroph**•ic

cat•bird

catch

catch•er

catch•y

cat•e•**gor**•i•cal

cat•e•go•rize

cat•e•go•ry

ca•ter

ca•ter•er

cat•er•pil•lar

cat•fish

ca•**thar**•sis

ca•**the**•dral

cath•ode-ray

Cath•o•lic

Ca•**thol**•i•cism

cat•nap

cat•nip

cat-o'-**nine**-tails

CAT scan

cat•sup

cat•tail

cat•tle

cat•ty

Cau•**ca**•sian

cau•cus

caught

caul•dron

cau•li•flow•er

caulk

cause

cause•way

caus•tic

cau•tion

cau•tion•ar•y

cau•tious

cav•al•**cade**

cav•a•**lier**

cav•al•ry

cave

cave-in

cave•man

cav•ern

cav•ern•ous

cave•wom•an

cav•i•ar

cav•i•ties

cav•i•ty

cease

cease-fire

cease•less

ceas•ing

ce•dar

ceil•ing

cel•e•brate

cel•e•brat•ing

cel•e•**bra**•tion

ce•**leb**•ri•ties

ce•**leb**•ri•ty

cel•er•y

ce•**les**•tial

cell (sounds like "sell")

The prisoner slept in his cell.

cel•lar

cel•list

cel•lo

cel•los

cel•lu•lar

cel•lu•loid

cel•lu•lose

Cel•si•us

Celt•ic

ce•**ment**

cem•e•ter•y

cen•sor

cen•sor•ship

cen•sure

cen•sur•ing

cen•sus

cent (sounds like "scent" and "sent")

A cent isn't worth much today.

cen•taur

cen•**ten**•ni•al

cen•ter

cen•ter•piece

cen•ti•grade

cen•ti•me•ter

cen•ti•pede

cen•tral

cen•**tri**•fu•gal

cen•**trip**•e•tal

cen•tu•ries

cen•**tu**•ri•on

cen•tu•ry

ce•**ram**•ic

ce•**ram**•ics

ce•re•al (sounds like "serial")

I eat two bowls of cereal every morning.

cer•e•**bel**•lum

ce•**re**•bral

cer•e•**mo**•ni•al

cer•e•mo•nies

cer•e•**mo**•ni•ous

cer•e•mo•ny

cer•tain

cer•tain•ty

cer•**tif**•i•cate

cer•ti•fi•**ca**•tion

cer•ti•fied
cer•ti•fies
cer•ti•fy
cer•ti•fy•ing
chafe
chaf•ing
cha•**grin**
chain
chair
chair•lift
chair•man
chair•per•son
chair•wom•an
cha•let
chal•ice
chalk
chalk•board
chalk•y
chal•lenge
cham•ber
cha•**me**•le•on
cham•ois
cham•**pagne**
cham•pi•on
cham•pi•on•ship
chance
chan•cel•lor
chanc•ing
chan•de•**lier**
change
change•a•**bil**•i•ty
change•a•ble
chan•nel
chant

Cha•nu•kah (*or*
  Ha•nuk•kah)
cha•os
cha•**ot**•ic
chap
chap•el
chap•lain
chaps

(**chaps**)

chap•ter
char•ac•ter
char•ac•ter•**is**•tic
char•ac•ter•i•**za**•tion
char•ac•ter•ize
cha•**rade**
char•coal
charge
charg•ing
char•i•ot
char•i•ot•**eer**
cha•**ris**•ma

char•i•ta•ble
char•i•ties
char•i•ty
charm
charm•ing
chart
char•ter
chase
chas•ing
chasm
chas•sis
chas•**tise**
  also pronounced
  chas•tise
chat
châ•**teau**
chat•ted
chat•ter
chat•ting
chat•ty
chauf•feur
  also pronounced
  chauf•**feur**
chau•vin•ist
cheap
cheap•en
cheat
cheat•ed
cheat•ing
check
check•book
check•er•board
check•ers
check•out

check•room
check•up
cheek
cheek•y
cheer
cheer•ful
cheer•ful•ly
cheer•i•ly
cheer•lead•er
cheer•less
cheer•y
cheese
chees•y
chee•tah
chef
chem•i•cal
chem•ist
chem•is•try
che•mo•**ther**•a•py
che•**nille**
cher•ish
Cher•o•kee
cher•ry
cher•ub
chess
chess•board
chest
chest•nut
chew
chew•ing
chew•ing **gum**
chew•y
Chey•**enne**
Chi•**ca**•go

Chi•**ca**•na
Chi•**ca**•no
chick
chick•a•dee
chick•en
chick•en **pox**
chick•pea
chic•o•ry
chide
chid•ing
chief
chiefs
chief•tain
chif•**fon**
chig•ger

Chihuahua

Chi•**hua**•hua
child
child•bear•ing
child•birth
child•hood
child•ish

chil•dren
Chi•le
chil•i (sounds like "chilly")
This chili has two kinds of beans.
chill
chill•i•ness
chill•y (sounds like "chili")
Take a sweater; it's chilly.
chime
chim•ing
chim•ney
chim•pan•**zee**
also pronounced chim•**pan**•zee
chin
chi•na
Chi•na
Chi•na•town
chin•**chil**•la
Chi•**nese**
chink
chinned
chin•ning
Chi•**nook**
chip
chip•munk
chipped
Chip•pe•wa
chip•ping
chi•ro•prac•tor
chirp

chis•el

chis•el•er

chiv•al•rous

chiv•al•ry

chlo•rine

chlo•ro•**fluor**•o•
car•bon

chlo•ro•form

chlo•ro•phyll

choc•o•late

Choc•taw

choice

choic•est

choir

choke

chok•ing

chol•e•ra

cho•**les**•ter•ol

choose

choos•ing

chop

chopped

chop•per

chop•ping

chop•py

chop•sticks

cho•ral

chord (sounds like
"cord")

*Play this chord on
the piano.*

chore

cho•re•**og**•ra•pher

cho•re•**og**•ra•phy

chor•tle

chort•ling

cho•rus

chose

cho•sen

chow•der

Christ

chris•ten•ing

Chris•tian

Chris•ti•**an**•i•ty

Christ•mas

chro•mo•some

chron•ic

chron•i•cal•ly

chron•i•cle

chron•i•cling

chron•o•**log**•i•cal

chrys•a•lis

chry•**san**•the•mum

chub•bi•er

chub•bi•est

chub•by

chuck

chuck•le

chuck•ling

chuck wag•on

chug

chum

chum•mi•ly

chum•my

chunk

chunk•y

church

church•go•er

church•yard

churl•ish

churn

chute (sounds like
"shoot")

*Throw the laundry
down the chute.*

chut•ney

ci•der

ci•**gar**

cig•a•**rette** (*or*
cig•a•**ret**)

cin•der

cin•e•ma

cin•na•mon

cir•ca

cir•cle

cir•cling

cir•cuit

cir•cu•lar

cir•cu•late

cir•cu•lat•ing

cir•cu•**la**•tion

cir•cu•la•to•ry

cir•**cum**•fer•ence

cir•cum•spect

cir•cum•stance

cir•cus

ci•**ta**•tion

cite (sounds like "sight"
and "site")

*Can you cite
Shakespeare on the
subject of love?*

cit•ies

cit•i•zen
cit•i•zen•ship
cit•rus
cit•y
civ•ic
civ•ics
civ•il
ci•**vil**•ian
civ•i•li•**za**•tion
civ•i•lize
civ•i•**liz**•ing
clad
claim
clam
clam•bake
clam•mi•ness
clam•my
clam•or
clamp
clan
clap
clap•board
clapped
clap•ping
clap•trap
clar•i•fi•**ca**•tion
clar•i•fied
clar•i•fies
clar•i•fy
clar•i•**net**
clar•i•ty
clash
clasp
class

clas•sic
clas•si•cal
clas•si•fied
clas•si•fies
clas•si•fy
class•mate
class•room
clas•sy
clat•ter
clause (sounds like "claws")
This sentence has a dependent clause.
claus•tro•**pho**•bi•a
claw
claws (sounds like "clause")
The cat dug its claws into the curtains.
clay
clean
clean•li•ness
cleanse
cleans•er
clear
clear•ance
clear•ing
clef
cleft
clem•en•cy
clem•ent
clench
Cle•o•**pat**•ra
cler•gy

cler•i•cal
clerk
clev•er
cli•**ché**
click
cli•ent
cli•en•**tele**
cliff
cliff-han•ger
cli•mate
cli•max
climb
clinch
clinch•er
cling
clin•ic
clin•i•cal
cli•**ni**•cian
clip
clip art
clip•board
clipped
clip•per
clip•ping
clique
cloak
cloak•room
clob•ber
clock
clock•wise
clock•work
clod
clog
clois•ter

clone

close

closed-cir·cuit

clos·et

close-up

clot

cloth (n.)

clothe (v.)

clothes

clothes·line

cloth·ing

cloud

cloud·burst

cloud·i·ness

cloud·y

clove

clo·ver

clown

clown·ish

cloy·ing

club

clue

clump

clum·si·ly

clum·si·ness

clum·sy

clus·ter

clutch

clut·ter

coach

coach·man

co·ag·u·late

co·ag·u·lat·ing

coal

co·a·li·tion

coarse (sounds like "course")

This material is coarse and scratchy.

coast

coast guard

coast·line

coat

coat·ing

coat of arms

coat·room

coax

co·balt

cob·bler

cob·ble·stone

co·bra

cob·web

co·caine

cock

cock·a·too

cockatoo

cock·er span·iel

cock·pit

cock·roach

cock·y

co·coa

co·co·nut

co·coon

cod·dle

cod·dling

code

co·ed·u·ca·tion

co·erce

co·erc·ing

co·er·cion

co·er·cive

cof·fee

cof·fin

cog

co·her·ent

coil

coin

co·in·cide

co·in·ci·dence

co·in·ci·den·tal

col·an·der

cold

cold·er

cold·est

cold-blood·ed

cole·slaw

col·i·se·um

col·lab·o·rate

col·lab·o·rat·ing

col·lab·o·ra·tion

col•**lage**
col•**lapse**
col•**laps**•i•ble
col•**laps**•ing
col•lar
col•lards
col•league
col•**lect**
col•**lec**•tion
col•lege
col•**lide**
col•**lid**•ing
col•lie
col•**li**•sion
col•**lo**•qui•al
col•**lo**•qui•al•ism
co•**logne**
co•lon
colo•nel
co•**lo**•ni•al
col•o•nies
col•on•ist
col•o•nize
col•o•ny
col•or
Col•o•**ra**•do
col•or•ful
col•or•ing
col•or•ize
col•or•less
co•**los**•sal
colt
col•um•bine
Co•**lum**•bus **Day**

col•umn
col•um•nist
co•ma
comb
com•bat
com•bi•**na**•tion
com•**bine**
com•**bin**•ing
com•**bus**•ti•ble
com•**bus**•tion
come
co•**me**•di•an

(comedian)

com•e•dies
com•e•dy
com•et
com•fort
com•fort•a•ble
com•ic
com•i•cal

com•ic **book**
com•ic **strip**
com•ma
com•**mand**
com•**mand**•er
com•**mand**•ment
com•**man**•do
com•**mem**•o•rate
com•**mem**•o•rat•ing
com•mem•o•**ra**•tion
com•**mence**
com•**mence**•ment
com•**menc**•ing
com•**mend**
com•**mend**•a•ble
com•men•**da**•tion
com•ment
com•men•tar•y
com•men•ta•tor
com•merce
com•**mer**•cial
com•**mer**•cial•ize
com•**mis**•er•ate
com•**mis**•er•at•ing
com•mis•er•**a**•tion
com•**mis**•sion
com•**mit**
com•**mit**•ment
com•**mit**•ted
com•**mit**•tee
com•**mod**•i•ty
com•mon
com•mon
  de•**nom**•i•na•tor

com·mon·ly
Com·mon Mar·ket
com·mon·place
com·mon sense
com·mon·wealth
com·mo·tion
com·mu·nal
com·mune (n.)
com·mune (v.)
com·mu·ni·ca·ble
com·mu·ni·cate
com·mu·ni·cat·ing
com·mu·ni·ca·tion
Com·mun·ion
com·mu·ni·qué
com·mun·ism
Com·mun·ist Par·ty
com·mu·ni·ties
com·mu·ni·ty
com·mut·er
com·pact (n.)
com·pact (v.)
com·pa·nies
com·pan·ion
com·pa·ny
com·pa·ra·ble
com·par·a·tive
com·pare
com·par·ing
com·par·i·son
com·part·ment
com·pass
com·pas·sion
com·pas·sion·ate

com·pat·i·ble
com·pel
com·pelled
com·pel·ling
com·pen·sate
com·pen·sat·ing
com·pen·sa·tion
com·pete
com·pe·tent
com·pet·ing
com·pe·ti·tion
com·pet·i·tive
com·pet·i·tor
com·pile
com·pla·cent
com·plain
com·plaint
com·ple·ment (sounds
   like "compliment")
*Ice cream will
complement the pie.*
com·plete
com·plet·ing
com·ple·tion
com·plex (adj.)
com·plex (n.)
com·plex·ion
com·plex·i·ty
com·pli·cate
com·pli·cat·ed
com·pli·cat·ing
comp·li·ca·tion
com·plied
com·plies

com·pli·ment (sounds
   like "complement")
*Thanks for the
flattering compliment.*
com·pli·men·ta·ry
com·ply
com·po·nent
com·pose
com·pos·ing
com·pos·ite
com·po·si·tion
com·post
com·po·sure
com·pound (adj. and n.)
com·pound (v.)
com·pre·hend
com·pre·hen·sion
com·pre·hen·sive
com·press (v.)
com·press (n.)
com·prise
com·pris·ing
com·pro·mise
com·pro·mis·ing
com·pul·so·ry
com·pu·ta·tion
com·pute
com·put·er
com·put·ing
com·rade
con·cave
con·ceal
con·cede
con·ced·ing

con•**ceit**
con•**ceit**•ed
con•**ceive**
con•**ceiv**•ing
con•cen•trate
con•cen•trat•ing
con•cen•**tra**•tion
con•**cen**•tric
con•cept
con•**cern**
con•**cerned**
con•**cern**•ing
con•cert
con•**cer**•to
con•**ces**•sion
conch
con•**cise**
con•**clude**
con•**clud**•ing
con•**clu**•sion
con•**coct**
con•cord
con•crete
con•**cur**
con•**curred**
con•**cus**•sion
con•**demn**
con•dem•**na**•tion
con•den•**sa**•tion
con•**dense**
con•**dens**•ing
con•de•**scend**•ing
con•**di**•tion
con•**di**•tion•al

con•**di**•tion•er
con•**do**•lence
con•do•**min**•i•um
con•dor
con•duct (n.)

(**conch**)

con•**duct** (v.)
con•**duc**•ting
con•**duc**•tor
cone
con•**fed**•er•a•cies
con•**fed**•er•a•cy
con•**fed**•er•ate
con•fed•er•**a**•tion
con•**fer**
con•fer•ence
con•**ferred**
con•**fer**•ring
con•**fess**
con•**fet**•ti
con•**fide**
con•fi•dence
con•fi•dent

con•fi•**den**•tial
con•**fid**•ing
con•**fine**
con•**fin**•ing
con•**firm**
con•fir•**ma**•tion
con•fis•cate
con•fis•cat•ing
con•fla•**gra**•tion
con•flict (n.)
con•**flict** (v.)
con•flu•ence
con•**form**
con•**form**•ing
con•**form**•ist
con•**front**
con•fron•**ta**•tion
Con•**fu**•cian•ism
Con•**fu**•cius
con•**fuse**
con•**fus**•ing
con•**fu**•sion
con•**ge**•ni•al
con•ge•ni•**al**•i•ty
con•**ges**•ted
con•**ges**•tion
con•**glom**•er•ate
con•glom•er•**a**•tion
con•**grat**•u•late
con•**grat**•u•lat•ing
con•grat•u•**la**•tions
con•gre•gate
con•gre•gat•ing
con•gre•**ga**•tion

Con•gress
con•**gres**•sio•nal
con•**gru**•ent
con•i•fer
con•ju•gate
con•ju•gat•ing
con•ju•**ga**•tion
con•**junc**•tion
con•jure
con•jur•er (*or*
  con•jur•or)
con•jur•ing
con•**nect**
Con•**nect**•i•cut
con•**nec**•tion
con•**nec**•tive
con•**nive**
con•**niv**•ing
con•nois•**seur**
con•quer
con•quest
con•science
con•sci•**en**•tious
con•scious
con•**sec**•u•tive
con•**sen**•sus
con•**sent**
con•se•quence
con•ser•**va**•tion
con•**serv**•a•tive
con•**serv**•a•to•ry
con•**serve**
con•**serv**•ing
con•**sid**•er

con•**sid**•er•a•ble
con•**sid**•er•ate
con•sid•er•**a**•tion
con•**sign**•ment
con•**sist**
con•**sis**•tent
con•sole (v.)
con•sole (n.)
con•**sol**•i•date
con•**sol**•i•dat•ing
con•sol•i•**da**•tion
con•**sol**•ing
con•so•nant
con•**spic**•u•ous
con•**spir**•a•cies
con•**spir**•a•cy
con•**spire**
con•**spir**•ing
con•sta•ble
con•stant
Con•stan•ti•**no**•ple
con•stel•**la**•tion
con•ster•**na**•tion
con•sti•pat•ed
con•sti•**pa**•tion
con•**stit**•u•ent
con•**stit**•u•en•cies
con•**stit**•u•en•cy
con•sti•tute
con•sti•tut•ing
con•sti•**tu**•tion
con•sti•**tu**•tion•al
con•**straint**
con•**strict**

con•**stric**•tion
con•**struct**
con•**struc**•tion
con•**struc**•tive
con•sul
con•sul•ar
con•sul•ate
con•**sult**
con•**sul**•tant
con•sul•**ta**•tion
con•**sume**
con•**sum**•er
con•**sum**•ing
con•**sump**•tion
con•tact
con•tact **lens**
con•**ta**•gious
con•**tain**
con•**tain**•er
con•**tam**•i•nate
con•**tam**•i•nat•ing
con•tam•i•**na**•tion
con•tem•plate
con•tem•plat•ing
con•tem•**pla**•tion
con•**tem**•po•rar•y
con•**tempt**
con•**tempt**•i•ble
con•**tend**
con•tent (n.)
con•**tent** (v. and adj.)
con•**tent**•ed
con•**tent**•ment
con•tents

con•test (n.)
con•test (v.)
con•tes•tant
con•text
con•ti•nent
con•ti•nen•tal
con•tin•u•al
con•tin•ue
con•tin•u•ing
con•ti•nu•i•ty
con•tin•u•ous
con•tort
con•tor•tion
con•tract (n.)
con•tract (v.)
con•trac•tion
con•tra•dict
con•tra•dic•tion
con•tra•dic•to•ry
con•trap•tion
con•trar•i•ness
con•trar•y
con•trast (n.)
con•trast (v.)
con•tri•bute
con•tri•but•ing
con•tri•bu•tion
con•trite
con•triv•ance
con•trive
con•triv•ing
con•trol
con•trolled
con•trol•ling

con•tro•ver•sial
con•tro•ver•sies
con•tro•ver•sy
con•va•lesce
con•va•les•cence
con•va•les•cent
con•va•lesc•ing
con•vec•tion
con•vene
con•ven•ience
con•ven•ient
con•vent
con•ven•tion
con•ven•tion•al
con•ven•tion•al•i•ty
con•verge
con•ver•gence
con•verg•ing
con•ver•sa•tion
con•ver•sa•tion•al
con•verse
con•vers•ing
con•ver•sion
con•vert
con•vert•i•ble
con•vex
  also pronounced
  con•vex
con•vey
con•vey•ance
con•vey•or belt
con•vict (v.)
con•vict (n.)
con•vic•tion

con•vince
con•vinc•ing
con•viv•i•al
con•vo•ca•tion
con•vok•ing
con•voy
con•vulse
con•vul•sion
coo
coo•ing
cook
cook•book
cook•ie
cool
cool•er
cool•ly
coop
co-op
co•op•er•ate

convict

co•**op**•er•at•ing
co•op•er•**a**•tion
co•**op**•er•a•tive
co•**or**•di•nate
co•**or**•di•nat•ed
co•**or**•di•nat•ing
co•**or**•di•**na**•tion
co•**or**•di•na•tor
cope
Co•pen•**ha**•gen
Co•**per**•ni•cus
cop•ied
cop•ies
co•pi•lot
cop•ing
co•pi•ous
cop•per
cop•per•head
cop•y
cop•y•ing
cop•y•right
cor•al
cord (sounds like
    "chord")
   *Please tie this cord
   to the post.*
cor•dial
cor•**dial**•i•ty
cor•dial•ly
cor•don
cor•du•roy
core
cork
cork•screw

corn
cor•ne•a
cor•ner
cor•ner•stone
cor•**net**
corn•flow•er
cor•nice
corn•meal
corn•row
corn•starch
co•**ro**•na
cor•o•nar•ies
cor•o•nar•y
cor•o•**na**•tion
cor•o•ner
cor•o•**net**
cor•po•ral
cor•po•**ra**•tion
corps
corpse
cor•pu•lence
cor•pu•lent
cor•pus•cle
cor•pus de•**lic**•ti
cor•**ral**
cor•**rect**
cor•**rec**•tion
cor•re•late
cor•re•lat•ing
cor•re•**la**•tion
cor•res•**pond**
cor•res•**pond**•ence
cor•res•**pond**•ent
cor•ri•dor

cor•**rode**
cor•**rod**•ing
cor•**ro**•sion
cor•**ro**•sive
cor•ru•gat•ed
cor•**rupt**
cor•**rupt**•i•ble
cor•**rup**•tion
cor•**sage**
cor•set
cos•**met**•ic
cos•mic
cos•mo•naut
cos•mo•**pol**•i•tan
cos•mos
cost
co-star
cost•ly
cos•tume
cot
cot•tage
cot•ton
cot•ton•mouth
cot•ton•tail
cot•ton•wood
couch
cou•gar
cough
could
could•n't
coun•cil (sounds like
    "counsel")
   *The city council passed
   the law.*

c

coun•sel (sounds like
"council")
*I will seek my
grandfather's counsel.*
coun•se•lor
count
count•down
coun•te•nance
coun•ter
coun•ter•**act**
coun•ter•**clock**•wise
coun•ter•feit
coun•ter•part
coun•ter•point
count•ess
coun•ties
coun•tries
coun•try
coun•try•side
coun•ty
cou•ple
cou•plet
cou•pling
cou•pon
cour•age
cou•**ra**•geous
cour•i•er
course (sounds like
"coarse")
*Math is her favorite
course.*
court
cour•te•ous
cour•te•sies

cour•te•sy
court•house
court•ly
court•room
court•ship
court•yard
cous•in
cove
cov•er
cov•er•age
cov•ered **wag**•on
co•vert
cov•et
cow
cow•ard
cow•ard•ice
cow•boy
cow•er
cow•girl
cow•hand
cow•hide
coy•**o**•te
also pronounced
coy•ote
co•zi•ly
co•zy
crab
crab•by
crack
crack•down
crack•er
crack•le
crack•ling
cra•dle

craft
craft•i•er
craft•i•est
craft•i•ly
crafts•per•son
craft•y
crag
cram
crammed
cram•ming
cramp
cramped
cran•ber•ries
cran•ber•ry
crane
crank
crank•i•er
crank•i•est
crank•i•ness
crank•y
crash
crass
crate
cra•ter
crat•ing
cra•**vat**
crave
crav•ing
crawl
cray•fish
cray•on
craze
cra•zi•er

cra•zi•est

cra•zi•ly

cra•zi•ness

cra•zy

creak (sounds like "creek")

I oiled that noisy creak.

cream

cream•er•y

crease

creas•ing

cre•**ate**

cre•**at**•ing

cre•**a**•tion

cre•**a**•tive

cre•a•**tiv**•i•ty

crea•ture

crèche

cre•**den**•tials

cred•i•**bil**•i•ty

cred•i•ble

cred•it

cred•it **card**

creed

creek (sounds like "creak")

He fell into the creek and got all wet.

creep

creep•y

cre•mate

cre•**ma**•tion

Cre•ole

crepe

crepe **pa**•per

crept

cres•cent

crescent

crest

crest•fall•en

crev•ice

crew

crib

crick•et

cried

cries

crime

crim•i•nal

crim•i•**nol**•o•gist

crim•i•**nol**•o•gy

crim•son

cringe

cring•ing

crin•kle

crin•kling

crin•o•line

crip•ple

crip•pled

crip•pling

cri•ses

cri•sis

crisp

criss•cross

crit•ic

crit•i•cal

crit•i•cism

crit•i•cize

crit•i•ciz•ing

cri•**tique**

croak

cro•**chet**

crock•er•y

croc•o•dile

cro•cus

crook

crook•ed

crop

cropped

crop•ping

cro•**quet** (often confused with "croquette")

They're playing croquet on the lawn.

cro•**quette** (often confused with "croquet")

This fish croquette is delicious.

cross
cross•bow
cross•breed
cross-coun•try
cross-ex•am•ine
cross-ref•er•ence
cross•roads
cross•walk
cross•word puz•zle
crouch
croup
crou•ton
crow
crow•bar
crowd
crown
cru•cial
cru•ci•ble
cru•ci•fied
cru•ci•fies
cru•ci•fix•ion
cru•ci•fy
cru•ci•fy•ing
crude
cru•el
cru•el•ty
cruise
cruis•er
cruis•ing
crumb
crum•ble
crum•bling
crum•ple
crum•pling

crunch
cru•sade
cru•sad•er
cru•sad•ing
crush
crust
crus•ta•cean
crutch
cry

cry

cry•ing
crys•tal
crys•tal•line
crys•tal•lize
cub
cube
cub•ing
cu•bic
cu•bi•cle
cu•bit

cuck•oo
cu•cum•ber
cud
cud•dle
cud•dling
cue (sounds like "queue")
He forgot his cue in the play.
cuff
cu•ing
cui•sine
cul-de-sac
cu•li•nar•y
cul•mi•nate
cul•mi•nat•ing
cul•mi•na•tion
cul•prit
cult
cul•ti•vate
cul•ti•vat•ing
cul•ti•va•tion
cul•tur•al
cul•ture
cul•tured
cum•ber•some
cun•ning
cum lau•de
cu•mu•late
cu•mu•lat•ing
cu•mu•la•tion
cu•mu•la•tive
cup
cup•board

cup·cake
cup·ful
Cu·pid
cupped
cup·ping
cur·a·ble
cu·rate
cu·ra·tor
  also pronounced
  cu·**ra**·tor
curb
curb·stone
curd
cur·dle
cur·dling
cure
cure-all
cur·few
cur·ing
cu·ri·**os**·i·ties
cu·ri·**os**·i·ty
cu·ri·ous
curl
cur·li·cue
curl·i·er
curl·i·est
curl·y
cur·rant (sounds like
  "current")
  *I made this currant
  jam myself.*

cur·ren·cy
cur·rent (sounds like
  "currant")
  *Electrical current runs
  through the wire.*
cur·**ric**·u·la
cur·**ric**·u·lum
cur·**ric**·u·lums
cur·ried
cur·ry
curse
curs·ing
cur·sor
cur·so·ry
cur·**tail**
cur·tain
curt
curt·sied
curt·sies
curt·sy
curve
curv·ing
cush·ion
cus·tard
cus·**to**·di·an
cus·to·dy
cus·tom
cus·tom·ar·y
cus·tom·er
cus·tom·ize
cus·tom-**made**

cut
cut·a·way
cute
cu·ti·cle
cut·lass
cut·le·ry
cut·ting
cy·ber·space
cy·cle
cy·cling
cy·clist
cy·clone
cy·clo·**ra**·ma
cyg·net
cyl·in·der
cym·bal (sounds like
  "symbol")
  *Strike that cymbal
  loudly.*
cyn·ic
cyn·i·cal
cyn·i·cism
cy·press
cyst
cy·to·plasm
czar (*or* tsar)
cza·**ri**·na (*or* tsa·**ri**·na)
Czech·o·slo·**va**·ki·a

dab

dabbed

dab·bing

dab·ble

dab·bling

dachs·hund

dad

dad·dies

dad·dy

dad·dy-**long**·legs

daf·fo·dil

daft

dag·ger

dai·ly

dain·ti·er

dain·ti·est

dain·ti·ly

dain·ti·ness

dain·ty

dair·ies

dair·y

dai·sies

dai·sy

dale

dal·lied

dal·lies

dal·ly

dal·ly·ing

dal·**ma**·tian

dam

dam·age

dam·aged

dam·ag·ing

Da·**mas**·cus

damp

damp·en

dam·sel

dance

danc·ing

dan·de·li·on

dan·di·er

dan·di·est

dan·druff

dan·dy

dan·ger

dan·ger·ous

dan·gle

dan·gling

dank

dap·ple

dap·pled

dap·pling

dare

dar·ing

dare·dev·il

dark

dark·en

dark·ness

dark·room

dar·ling

darn

dart

dash

dash·board

da·ta

da·ta·base

date

dat·ing

daugh·ter

daugh·ter-in-law

daugh·ters-in-law

daunt

daunt·ing

daunt·less

daw·dle

daw·dler

daw·dling

dawn

day

day·break

day care

day·dream

day·light

day·time

daze

daz·ing

daz·zle

daz·zling

dea·con

dead

dead·en

dead end

dead·line

dead·lock

dead·ly

deaf

deaf·en
deaf·en·ing
deaf·ness
deal
deal·er
dear
death
death·bed
death·ly
death·trap
de·**ba**·cle
de·**bate**
de·**bat**·ing
deb·it
deb·o·**nair**

debonair

de·**bris**
debt
debt·or
de·**bug**

de·**but**
  also pronounced
  de·but
deb·u·tante
dec·ade
dec·a·dence
dec·a·dent
de·**caf**·fein·at·ed
de·cal
de·**cant**·er
de·**cap**·i·tate
de·**cap**·i·tat·ing
de·cap·i·**ta**·tion
de·**cath**·lon
de·**cay**
de·**ceased**
de·**ceit**
de·**ceit**·ful
de·**ceive**
de·**ceiv**·ing
De·**cem**·ber
de·cen·cy
de·cent
de·**cen**·tral·ize
de·**cep**·tion
de·**cep**·tive
dec·i·bel
de·**cide**
de·**cid**·ed
de·**cid**·ing
de·**cid**·u·ous
dec·i·mal
de·**ci**·pher
de·**ci**·sion

de·**ci**·sive
deck
dec·la·**ra**·tion
Dec·la·**ra**·tion of
  In·de·**pend**·ence
de·**clare**
de·**clar**·ing
de·**cline**
de·**clin**·ing
de·**code**
de·**cod**·ing
de·com·**pose**
de·com·**pos**·ing
de·con·**ges**·tant
de·con·**tam**·i·nate
de·con·**tam**·i·nat·ing
de·con·tam·i·**na**·tion
dec·o·rate
dec·o·rat·ing
dec·o·**ra**·tion
de·cou·**page**
de·coy
de·**crease** (v.)
de·crease (n.)
de·**creas**·ing
de·**cree**
de·**cree**·ing
de·**crep**·it
de·**cried**
de·**cries**
de·**cry**
de·**cry**·ing
ded·i·cate
ded·i·cat·ing

ded•i•**ca**•tion
de•**duce**
de•**duc**•ing
de•**duct**
de•**duct**•i•ble
de•**duc**•tion
deed
deep
deep-seat•ed
deer
deer•skin
de•**face**
de•**fac**•ing
de•**feat**
de•**fect**
de•**fec**•tion
de•**fend**
de•**fend**•ant
de•**fense**
de•**fense**•less
de•**fen**•sive
de•**fer**
de•**ferred**
de•**fi**•ance
de•**fi**•ant
de•**fi**•cien•cies
de•**fi**•cien•cy
de•**fi**•cient
def•i•cit
de•**fied**
de•**fies**
de•**fine**
def•i•nite
def•i•**ni**•tion

de•**flate**
de•**flect**
de•for•est•**a**•tion
de•for•**ma**•tion
de•**formed**
de•**for**•mi•ty
de•**fraud**
de•**frost**
deft
de•**fuse**

defuse

de•**fus**•ing
de•**fy**
de•**gen**•er•ate
de•**gen**•er•at•ing
de•gen•er•**a**•tion
deg•ra•**da**•tion
de•**grade**
de•**grad**•ing
de•**gree**
de•**hy**•drate

de•**hy**•drat•ing
de•hy•**dra**•tion
de•i•ties
de•i•ty
de•**ject**•ed
de•**jec**•tion
Del•a•ware
de•**lay**
de•**lec**•ta•ble
del•e•gate
del•e•gat•ing
del•e•**ga**•tion
de•**lete**
de•**let**•ing
de•**lib**•er•ate
de•**lib**•er•at•ing
de•**lib**•er•**a**•tion
del•i•cate
del•i•ca•**tes**•sen
de•**li**•cious
de•**light**
de•**light**•ful
de•**light**•ful•ly
de•**lin**•quen•cy
de•**lin**•quent
de•**lir**•i•ous
de•**lir**•i•um
de•**liv**•er
de•**liv**•er•y
del•ta
de•**lude**
de•**lud**•ing
del•uge
de•**lu**•sion

de·**mand**
de·**mand**·ing
de·**mean**
de·**ment**·ed
de·**mer**·it
de·**mise**
dem·o
de·**moc**·ra·cies
de·**moc**·ra·cy
dem·o·crat
dem·o·**crat**·ic
Dem·o·**crat**·ic **Par**·ty
de·mo·**graph**·ics
de·**mol**·ish
dem·o·**li**·tion
de·mon
de·**mon**·ic
dem·on·strate
dem·on·strat·ing
dem·on·**stra**·tion
dem·**on**·stra·tive
de·**mor**·al·ized
den
de·**nied**
de·**nies**
den·im
Den·mark
de·**nom**·i·**na**·tion
de·**nom**·i·na·tor
de·**note**
de·**not**·ing
de·**nounce**
de·**noun**·ced
de·**nounc**·ing

dense
den·si·ty
dent
den·tal
den·tist
den·tist·ry
den·ture
de·**ny**
de·**ny**·ing
de·**o**·dor·ant
de·**o**·dor·ize
de·**part**
de·**part**·ment
de·part·**men**·tal
de·**par**·ture
de·**pend**
de·pend·a·**bil**·i·ty
de·**pend**·a·ble
de·**pend**·ence
de·**pend**·ent
de·**pict**
de·**plete**
de·**plet**·ing
de·**ple**·tion
de·**plor**·a·ble
de·**plore**
de·**plor**·ing
de·**ploy**
de·**ploy**·ment
de·**port**
de·**port**·ment
de·**pos**·it
de·**pos**·i·tor
de·**pos**·i·tor·y

de·pot
de·**praved**
de·**prav**·i·ty
de·**pre**·ci·ate
de·**pre**·ci·at·ing
de·**pressed**
de·**pres**·sion
dep·ri·**va**·tion
de·**prive**
de·**priv**·ing
depth
dep·u·tize
dep·u·ties
dep·u·ty
de·**rail**·ment
de·**ranged**
der·bies
der·by
der·e·lict
der·e·**lic**·tion
de·**ride**
de·**rid**·ing
de·**ri**·sion
de·**rive**
de·**riv**·ing
der·ma·**tol**·o·gist
der·ma·**tol**·o·gy
de·**rog**·a·to·ry
der·rick
de·**scend**
de·**scend**·ant
des·**cent**
de·**scribe**
de·**scrib**·ing

de•**scrip**•tion
de•**scrip**•tive
de•**seg**•re•gate
de•**seg**•re•gat•ing
de•seg•re•**ga**•tion
des•ert (n.)

The Sahara is the world's largest desert.

de•**sert** (v.) (sounds like "dessert")

A loyal friend won't desert you.

de•**serve**
de•**serv**•ing
de•**sign**
des•ig•nate
des•ig•nat•ing
des•ig•**na**•tion
de•**sign**•er
de•**sign**•ing
de•**sire**
de•**sir**•ing
desk
desk•top
des•o•late
des•o•**la**•tion
de•**spair**
des•per•**a**•do
des•per•ate
des•per•**a**•tion
de•**spise**
de•**spis**•ing
de•**spite**
de•**spond**•ent

des•pot
des•**pot**•ic
des•pot•ism
des•**sert** (sounds like "desert")

I'd like chocolate pudding for dessert.

des•ti•**na**•tion
des•tined
des•ti•ny
des•ti•tute
des•ti•**tu**•tion
de•**stroy**
de•**stroy**•er
de•**struct**•i•ble
des•**truc**•tive
de•**tach**
de•**tached**
de•**tach**•ment
de•**tail**
de•**tain**
de•**tect**
de•**tec**•tive
de•**tec**•tor
de•**ten**•tion
de•**ter**
de•**ter**•gent
de•**te**•ri•o•rate
de•**te**•ri•o•rat•ing
de•te•ri•o•**ra**•tion
de•ter•mi•**na**•tion
de•**ter**•mine
de•**ter**•mined
de•**ter**•min•ing

de•**test**
det•o•nate
det•o•nat•ing
det•o•**na**•tion
de•tour
de•**tract**
de•**trac**•tion
det•ri•**men**•tal
De•**troit**
deuce
de•**val**•u•ate
de•val•u•**a**•tion
de•**val**•ue
dev•as•tate
dev•as•tat•ing
dev•as•**ta**•tion
de•**vel**•op
de•**vel**•op•ing
de•**vel**•op•ment
de•vi•ate
de•vi•at•ing
de•vi•**a**•tion
de•**vice**
dev•il
dev•il•ish
de•vi•ous
de•**vise**
de•**vote**
de•**vot**•ed
de•**vot**•ing
de•**vo**•tion
de•**vour**
dew (sounds like "due")

The dew on the grass is slippery.

dew•y

dex•**ter**•i•ty

dex•ter•ous

di•a•**be**•tes

di•a•**bet**•ic

di•a•**bol**•ic

di•ag•**nose**

di•ag•**nos**•ing

di•ag•**no**•sis

di•ag•**nos**•tic

di•ag•nos•**ti**•cian

di•**ag**•o•nal

di•a•gram

di•al

di•a•lect

di•a•logue

di•**al**•y•sis

di•**am**•e•ter

dia•mond

di•a•per

di•a•phragm

di•ar•**rhe**•a

di•a•ries

di•a•ry

dice

dic•tate

dic•tat•ing

dic•**ta**•tion

dic•ta•tor

dic•ta•**to**•ri•al

dic•tion•ar•ies

dic•tion•ar•y

did

did•n't

die (sounds like "dye")

You won't die if you eat asparagus.

died (sounds like "dyed")

Lincoln died in 1865.

die•sel

di•et

di•e•tar•y

di•e•**tet**•ic

dif•fer•ence

dif•fer•ent

dif•fi•cult

dif•fi•cul•ty

dig

(**dig**)

di•**gest** (v.)

di•gest (n.)

di•**gest**•i•ble

di•**ges**•tion

dig•it

dig•it•al

dig•i•tize

dig•ni•fied

dig•ni•fies

dig•ni•ty

di•**gress**

di•**gres**•sion

di•**lap**•i•dat•ed

di•lap•i•**da**•tion

di•late

di•**lat**•ing

di•**la**•tion

di•**lem**•ma

dil•i•gence

dil•i•gent

di•**lute**

di•**lut**•ing

di•**lu**•tion

dim

dime

di•**men**•sion

di•**min**•ish

dimmed

dim•ming

dim•ple

din

dine

din•er

di•**nette**

ding•bat

din•ghy (often
  confused with
  "dingy")
  Let's row to the island
  in the dinghy.
ding•i•er
ding•i•est
din•gy (often confused
  with "dinghy")
  She painted the dark,
  dingy room white.
din•ing
din•ing **room**
din•ner
di•no•saur
di•o•cese
dip
di•**plo**•ma
di•**plo**•ma•cy
dip•lo•mat
dip•lo•**mat**•ic
dipped
dip•per
dip•ping
dire
di•**rect**
di•**rec**•tion
di•**rec**•tor
di•**rec**•to•ries
di•**rec**•to•ry
di•**ri**•gi•ble
dirt
dir•ti•er
dir•ti•est

dir•ti•ness
dir•ty
dis
dis•a•**bil**•i•ty
dis•**a**•ble
dis•**a**•bled
dis•ad•**van**•tage
dis•a•**gree**
dis•a•**gree**•a•ble
dis•a•**gree**•ing
dis•a•**gree**•ment
dis•ap•**pear**
dis•ap•**pear**•ance
dis•ap•**point**
dis•ap•**point**•ment
dis•ap•**prov**•al
dis•ap•**prove**
dis•ap•**prov**•ing
dis•**arm**
dis•**ar**•ma•ment

dis•**as**•ter
dis•**as**•trous
dis•be•**lief**
dis•be•**lieve**
disc (or disk)
dis•**card**
dis•**charge** (v.)
dis•charge (n.)
dis•**charg**•ing
dis•**ci**•ple
dis•ci•pli•nar•y
dis•ci•pline
dis•ci•plin•ing
disc jock•ey
dis•**claim**
dis•**claim**•er
dis•**close**
dis•**clos**•ing
dis•**clo**•sure
dis•co
dis•**com**•fort
dis•con•**nect**
dis•con•**tent**•ed
dis•con•**tin**•ue
dis•con•**tin**•u•ing
dis•cord
dis•count
dis•**cour**•age
dis•**cour**•age•ment
dis•**cour**•ag•ing
dis•**cov**•er
dis•**creet**
dis•**crim**•i•nate
dis•**crim**•i•nat•ing

(**dirigible**)

dis•crim•i•**na**•tion

dis•cus (often confused with "discuss")

He threw the discus in the Olympics.

dis•**cuss** (often confused with "discus")

Let's discuss this matter later.

dis•**cus**•sion

dis•**ease**

dis•**fig**•ure

dis•**grace**

dis•**grace**•ful

dis•**grac**•ing

dis•**grun**•tled

dis•**guise**

dis•**guis**•ing

dis•**gust**•ing

dish

dish•es

di•**shev**•eled

dis•**hon**•est

dis•**hon**•or

dis•**hon**•or•able

dish•wash•er

dis•il•**lu**•sion

dis•in•**fect**

dis•in•**fect**•ant

dis•**in**•te•grate

dis•**in**•te•grat•ing

dis•**in**•te•**gra**•tion

dis•**in**•ter•est•ed

dis•**joint**•ed

disk or **disc**

dis•**like**

dis•**lo**•cate

also pronounced **dis**•lo•cate

dis•lo•**ca**•tion

dis•**lodge**

dis•**lodg**•ing

dis•mal

dis•**man**•tle

dis•**mayed**

dis•**miss**

dis•**miss**•al

dis•**mount**

dis•o•**be**•di•ent

dis•o•**bey**

dis•**or**•der•ly

dis•**or**•gan•ized

dis•**own**

dis•**patch**

dis•**pel**

dis•**pen**•sa•ble

dis•**pen**•sa•ries

dis•**pen**•sa•ry

dis•**pense**

dis•**place**

dis•**place**•ment

dis•**plac**•ing

dis•**play**

dis•**please**

dis•**pleas**•ing

dis•**pos**•a•ble

dis•**pos**•al

dis•**pose**

dis•po•**si**•tion

dis•**prove**

dis•**prov**•ing

dis•**pute**

dis•**put**•ing

dis•qual•i•fi•**ca**•tion

dis•**qual**•i•fied

dis•**qual**•i•fies

dis•**qual**•i•fy

dis•re•**gard**

dis•**rep**•u•ta•ble

dis•res•**pect**

dis•res•**pect**•ful

dis•res•**pect**•ful•ly

dis•**rupt**

dis•**rup**•tion

dis•**sat**•is•**fac**•tion

dis•**sat**•is•fied

dis•**sat**•is•fies

dis•**sat**•is•fy

dis•**sect**

dis•**sec**•tion

dis•**sem**•i•nate

dis•**sem**•i•nat•ing

dis•**sem**•i•**na**•tion

dis•**sen**•sion

dis•**sent**

dis•**serv**•ice

dis•si•dent

dis•**solve**

dis•**solv**•ing

dis•**suade**

dis•**suad**•ing

dis•tance
dis•tant
dis•taste
dis•taste•ful
dis•tem•per
dis•till
dis•til•la•tion
dis•till•er•y
dis•tinct
dis•tinc•tion
dis•tinc•tive
dis•tin•guish
dis•tin•guish•a•ble
dis•tin•guished
dis•tort
dis•tor•tion
dis•tract
dis•trac•tion
dis•tress
dis•trib•ute
dis•trib•ut•ing
dis•tri•bu•tion
dis•trib•u•tor
dis•trict
dis•trust
dis•turb
dis•turb•ance
dis•use
ditch
dit•to
dive
div•er
di•verse
di•ver•sion

di•ver•si•ty
di•vert
di•vide
di•vid•ed
div•i•dend
di•vid•ing
di•vine
div•ing
di•vis•i•ble
di•vi•sion
di•vi•sor
di•vorce
di•vorc•ing
di•vulge
di•vulg•ing
diz•zi•er
diz•zi•est
diz•zi•ness
diz•zy
do
Do•ber•man
  pin•scher
doc•ile
dock
dock•et
dock•yard
doc•tor
doc•tor•ate
doc•trine
doc•u•dra•ma
doc•u•ment
doc•u•men•ta•ries
doc•u•men•ta•ry
dodge

dodg•ing
doe (sounds like
  "dough")
  *Look at the beautiful
  doe in the woods.*
does
does•n't
dog
dog•house
dog•ma
dog•mat•ic
dog•wood
doi•lies
doi•ly
dole
doll
dol•lar
dol•phin
dome
do•mes•tic
do•mes•ti•cate
do•mes•ti•ca•tion
dom•i•nant
dom•i•nate
dom•i•nat•ing
dom•i•na•tion
do•min•ion
dom•i•no
dom•i•noes (or
  dom•i•nos)
don
do•nate
do•na•tion
done

don·key
donned
don·ning
do·nor
don't
do·nut (*or* **dough**·nut)
doo·dle
doo·dling
doom
dooms·day
door
door·bell
door·knob
door·man
door·step
door·way
dope
dor·mant
dor·mi·to·ries
dor·mi·to·ry
dos·age
dose
dot
dote
dot·ted
dot·ting
dou·ble
dou·ble-**cross**
dou·ble-**head**·er
doubt
dough (sounds like "doe")

I knead the dough to make bread.

dough·nut (*or* **do**·nut)
dove (rhymes with "love")

A dove is a bird.

dove (rhymes with "stove")

She dove into the pool.

down
down·cast
down·load

downpour

down·pour
down·right
downs
down·size
down·stairs (adv. and n.)
down·stairs (adj.)
down·stream
Down syn·drome (also called **Down's** syndrome)

down·town
doze
doz·en
doz·ing
drab
draft
drag
drag·on
drag·on·flies
drag·on·fly
drain
drain·age
drained
dra·ma
dra·**mat**·ic
dra·**mat**·i·cal·ly
dram·a·tize
drape
drap·ing
dras·tic
draw
draw·back
draw·bridge
drawer

The socks are in the top drawer.

draw·er

The talented drawer drew lovely pictures.

drawl
drawn
draw·string
dread
dread·ful

dread·locks
dream
dream·y
drear·y
dredge
dredg·ing
dregs
drench
dress
dress·er
dress·ing
drew
drib·ble
drib·bling
dried
dri·er (sounds like "dryer")

This shirt is drier than the other one.

dries
dri·est
drift
drift·wood
drill
dri·ly
drink
drip
dripped
drip·ping
drip·pings
drive
drive-in
driv·en
drive·way

driv·ing
driz·zle
driz·zling
driz·zly
drone
dron·ing
drool
droop
droop·ed
droop·ing
drop
dropped
drop·ping
drought
drove
drown
drows·i·er
drows·i·est
drow·si·ness
drow·sy
drudge
drudg·er·y
drug
drugged
drug·gist
drug·store
drum
drummed
drum·mer
drum·ming
drum·stick
drunk
dry

dry cell
dry-clean
dry·er (sounds like "drier")

Put the wet clothes into the dryer.

dry·ing
dual (sounds like "duel")

My new car has dual exhaust pipes.

du·bi·ous
duch·ess
duck
duct
dud
due (sounds like "dew")

The homework is due today.

drummer

duel (sounds like "dual")

The duel was fought at daybreak.

du•et

dug•out

duke

dull

dumb

dumb•bell

dumb•found•ed

dum•my

dump

dune

dun•ga•**ree**

dun•geon

du•plex

du•pli•cate

du•pli•cat•ing

du•pli•**ca**•tion

du•pli•ca•tor

du•ra•**bil**•i•ty

du•ra•ble

du•**ra**•tion

dur•ing

dusk

dusk•y

dust

dust•bin

dust•pan

dust•y

du•ties

du•ti•ful

du•ty

dwarf

dwarf•ish

dwarfs (*or* **dwarves**)

dwell

dwell•ing

dwin•dle

dwin•dling

dye (sounds like "die")

She will dye her shoes to match her dress.

dyed (sounds like "died")

She dyed her hair blonde.

dye•ing (sounds like "dying")

He's dyeing his shirt green.

dy•ing (sounds like "dyeing")

She's dying to meet the new boy.

dy•**nam**•ic

dy•na•mite

dy•na•mo

dy•na•mos

dy•nas•ties

dy•nas•ty

dys•**lex**•i•a

dys•**lex**•ic

dys•en•ter•y

each
ea·ger
ea·ger·ly
ea·gle
ear
ear·ache
ear·drum
ear·li·er
ear·li·est
ear·ly
ear·muffs
earn (sounds like
   "urn")

*How much will I earn
for this job?*

ear·nest
ear·phone
ear·ring
ear·shot
earth
earth·bound
earth·i·ness
earth·ling
earth·ly
earth·quake
earth·shak·ing
earth·worm
earth·y
ease
ea·sel
eas·i·er
eas·i·est

eas·i·ly
eas·i·ness
eas·ing
east
East·er
eas·y
eas·y·go·ing
eat
eat·a·ble
eaves
eaves·drop
eaves·drop·ping
ebb
eb·on·y
ec·**cen**·tric
ec·cen·**tric**·i·ty
ech·o
ech·oed
ech·oes
ech·o·ing
e·**clipse**
e·**clips**·ing
ec·o·**log**·i·cal
e·**col**·o·gist
e·**col**·o·gy
e·co·**nom**·i·cal
e·co·**nom**·ics
e·**con**·o·mist
e·**con**·o·mize
e·**con**·o·my
ec·o·sys·tem
ec·sta·sy

ec·**stat**·ic
Ec·ua·dor
ec·ze·ma
ed·dies
ed·dy
E·den
edge
edge·wise
edg·ing
edg·y
ed·i·ble
ed·i·fice
ed·it
ed·it·ing
e·**di**·tion
ed·i·tor
ed·i·**to**·ri·al
ed·i·**to**·ri·al·ize
ed·u·cate
ed·u·cat·ing
ed·u·**ca**·tion
ed·u·**ca**·tion·al·ly
ed·u·ca·tor
eel
ee·rie
ee·ri·er
ee·ri·est
ee·ri·ness
ef·**fect**
ef·**fec**·tive
ef·fer·**ves**·cence
ef·fer·**ves**·cent

ef•**fi**•cien•cy
ef•**fi**•cient
ef•fi•gy
ef•fort
egg
egg•head
egg•nog
egg•plant
egg•shell
e•go
e•go•**cen**•tric
e•go•tism
e•go•tist
e•go•**tis**•tic
e•gret
E•gypt
Eif•fel **Tow**•er
eight (sounds like
  "ate")
  *The cat had eight
  kittens.*
eigh•**teen**
eight•i•eth
eight•y
Ein•stein
Ei•sen•how•er
ei•ther
e•**ject**
e•**jec**•tion
e•**lab**•o•rate
e•**lab**•o•rat•ing
e•lab•o•**ra**•tion
e•**lapse**
e•**laps**•ing

e•**las**•tic
e•las•**tic**•i•ty
el•bow
el•der
el•der•ber•ries
el•der•ber•ry
eld•er•ly
eld•est
e•**lect**
e•**lec**•tion
e•**lec**•tive
e•**lec**•tor•ate
e•**lec**•tric
e•**lec**•tri•cal•ly
e•lec•**tri**•cian
e•lec•**tric**•ity
e•lec•tri•fi•**ca**•tion
e•**lec**•tri•fied
e•**lec**•tri•fies
e•**lec**•tri•fy

e•lec•tri•fy•ing
e•**lec**•tro•cute
e•lec•tro•**cu**•tion
e•**lec**•trode
e•lec•**trol**•y•sis
e•**lec**•tro•lyte
e•lec•tro•**mag**•net
e•lec•tro•**mag**•net•ism
e•**lec**•tron
e•lec•**tron**•ic
e•lec•**tron**•ics
el•e•gance
el•e•gant
el•e•gies
el•e•gy
el•e•ment
el•e•**men**•tal
el•e•**men**•ta•ry
el•e•phant
el•e•**phan**•tine
el•e•vate
el•e•**vat**•ing
el•e•**va**•tion
el•e•**va**•tor
e•**lev**•en
e•**lev**•enth
elf
el•i•gi•**bil**•i•ty
el•i•gi•ble
e•**lim**•i•nate
e•**lim**•i•nat•ing
e•**lim**•i•**na**•tion
e•**lite**
e•**lix**•ir

elf

E•liz•a•**be**•than
elk
el•**lipse**
elm
e•**lope**
e•**lope**•ment
e•**lop**•ing
el•o•quence
el•o•quent
else
else•where
e•**lude** (sounds like
   "allude")
   How long can the
   thief elude the police?
e•**lu**•sive
elves
e•**man**•ci•pate
e•**man**•ci•pat•ing
e•man•ci•**pa**•tion
e•**man**•ci•pa•tor
em•**balm**
em•**balm**•er
em•**bank**•ment
em•**bar**•go
em•**bar**•goes
em•**bark**
em•bar•**ka**•tion
em•**bar**•rass
em•**bar**•rass•ment
em•bas•sies
em•bas•sy
em•**bed**
em•**bel**•lish

em•**bel**•lish•ment
em•bers
em•**bez**•zle
em•**bez**•zler
em•**bit**•tered
em•blem
em•**bod**•ied
em•**bod**•ies
em•**bod**•i•ment
em•**bod**•y
em•**boss**
em•**brace**
em•**brace**•a•ble
em•**brac**•ing
em•**broi**•der
em•**broi**•der•y
em•bry•o
em•bry•os
em•er•ald
e•**mer**•gen•cy
em•i•grate
em•i•grat•ing
em•i•**gra**•tion
e•**mis**•sion
e•**mit**
e•**mit**•ted
e•**mit**•ting
e•**mote**
e•**mot**•ing
e•**mo**•tion
e•**mo**•tion•al
e•**mo**•tion•al•ism
e•**mo**•tion•al•ly
em•pa•thy

em•per•or
em•pha•sis
em•pha•size
em•pha•siz•ing
em•**phat**•ic
em•pire
em•**ploy**
em•**ploy**•ee
em•**ploy**•er

embrace

em•**ploy**•ment
em•press
emp•ti•ed
emp•ti•ness
emp•ty
emp•ty•ing
em•u•late
em•u•lat•ing
en•**a**•ble
en•**a**•bling
e•**nam**•el

e•**nam**•eled
en•**chant**
en•**chant**•ed
en•**chant**•ing
en•**chant**•ress
en•chil•**a**•da
en•**cir**•cle
en•**cir**•cling
en•**close**
en•**clos**•ing
en•**clo**•sure
en•**com**•pass
en•core
en•**coun**•ter
en•**cour**•age
en•**cour**•age•ment
en•**cour**•ag•ing
en•cy•clo•**pe**•di•a
end
en•**dan**•ger
en•**dan**•gered
en•**deav**•or
en•dive
end•less
en•**dor**•phin
en•**dorse**
en•**dorse**•ment
en•**dors**•ing
en•**dow**
en•**dow**•ment
en•**dure**
en•**dur**•ing
en•e•mies
en•e•my

en•er•**get**•ic
en•er•gize
en•er•gy
en•**force**
en•**force**•a•ble
en•**force**•ment
en•**forc**•ing
en•**gage**
en•**gage**•ment
en•**gag**•ing
en•gine
en•gi•**neer**
Eng•land
Eng•lish
en•**grave**
en•**grav**•ing
en•**gross**
en•**gross**•ing
en•**hance**
en•**hance**•ment
en•**hanc**•ing
e•**nig**•ma
en•ig•**mat**•ic
en•ig•**mat**•i•cal•ly
en•**joy**
en•**joy**•a•ble
en•**joy**•ment
en•**large**
en•**large**•ment
en•**larg**•ing
en•**light**•en
en•**light**•en•ment
en•**list**
en•**list**•ment

e•**nor**•mi•ty
e•**nor**•mous
e•**nough**
en•**rage**
en•**rag**•ing
en•**rich**
en•**rich**•ment
en•**roll**
en•**roll**•ment
en•route
en•**sem**•ble
en•**slave**
en•**slave**•ment
en•**tan**•gle
en•**tan**•gle•ment
en•ter
en•ter•prise
en•ter•pris•ing
en•ter•**tain**
en•ter•**tain**•ment
en•**thrall**
en•**thu**•si•asm
en•thu•si•**as**•tic
en•thu•si•**as**•ti•cal•ly
en•**tice**
en•**tice**•ment
en•**tic**•ing
en•**tire**
en•**tire**•ty
en•**trance**
en•**trap**
en•**trap**•ment
en•**trapped**
en•tre•pre•**neur**

en•tries
en•**trust**
en•try
e•**nun**•ci•ate
e•**nun**•ci•at•ing
e•nun•ci•**a**•tion
en•**vel**•op (v.)
en•ve•lope (n.)
en•**vel**•op•ing
en•vi•a•ble
en•vi•ous
en•**vi**•ron•ment
en•vi•ron•**men**•tal
en•vied
en•vies
en•vy
en•zyme
e•on
ep•ic
ep•i•cen•ter
ep•i•cure
ep•i•cu•**re**•an
ep•i•**dem**•ic
ep•i•**glot**•tis
ep•i•lep•sy
ep•i•logue
E•pis•co•**pa**•li•an
ep•i•sode
ep•i•taph
e•**pit**•o•mize
ep•och
e•qual
e•**qual**•i•ty
e•qual•ize

e•**quate**
e•**quat**•ing
e•**qua**•tion
e•**qua**•tor
e•qua•**to**•ri•al
e•**ques**•tri•an
e•qui•**lat**•er•al
e•qui•**lib**•ri•um
e•qui•nox
e•**quip**
e•**quip**•ment
e•**quipped**
e•**quip**•ping
e•**quiv**•a•lent
e•ra
e•**rase**
e•**ras**•er
e•**ras**•ing
e•**rect**
e•**rec**•tor
er•mine
e•**rode**
e•**rod**•ing
e•**ro**•sion
err
er•rand
er•**rat**•ic
erred
err•ing
er•ror
e•**rupt**
e•**rup**•tion
es•ca•late
es•ca•lat•ing

es•ca•la•tor
es•**cape**
es•**cap**•ing
es•**cort** (v.)
es•cort (n.)
Es•ki•mo
Es•ki•mos
e•**soph**•a•gus
es•**pe**•cial•ly
Es•pe•**ran**•to
es•pi•o•nage
es•pla•nade
es•say
es•say•ist
es•**sen**•tial
es•**tab**•lish
es•**tab**•lish•ment
es•ti•mate
es•ti•mat•ing
es•tu•ar•y
etc.
etch
e•**ter**•nal
e•**ter**•ni•ty
e•ther
eth•ics
E•thi•**o**•pi•a
eth•nic
et•i•quette
et•y•**mol**•o•gist
et•y•**mol**•o•gy
eu•ca•**lyp**•tus
eu•lo•gies
eu•lo•gy

eu•phe•mism
Eu•rope
Eu•ro•pe•an
eu•tha•na•sia
e•vac•u•ate
e•vac•u•at•ing
e•vac•u•a•tion
e•vade
e•vad•ing
e•val•u•ate
e•val•u•at•ing
e•val•u•a•tion
e•van•gel•i•cal
e•van•ge•list
e•vap•o•rate
e•vap•o•rat•ing
e•vap•o•ra•tion
eve
e•ven
eve•ning
e•vent
e•ven•tu•al
e•ven•tu•al•ly
ev•er
ev•er•glade
ev•er•green
ev•er•last•ing
eve•ry
eve•ry•bod•y
eve•ry•day
eve•ry•one
eve•ry•thing
eve•ry•where
e•vict

e•vic•tion
ev•i•dence
ev•i•dent
e•vil
e•vil-mind•ed
e•voke
e•vok•ing
ev•o•lu•tion
e•volve
e•volv•ing
ewe (sounds like "you")
   *A ewe is a female
   sheep.*

(**ewe**)

ex•act
ex•act•ly
ex•ag•ger•ate
ex•ag•ger•at•ing
ex•ag•ger•a•tion
ex•am

ex•am•in•a•tion
ex•am•ine
ex•am•in•ing
ex•am•ple
ex•as•per•ate
ex•as•per•at•ing
ex•as•per•a•tion
ex•ca•vate
ex•ca•vat•ing
ex•ca•va•tion
ex•ceed
ex•cel
ex•celled
ex•cel•lence
ex•cel•lent
ex•cel•ling
ex•cept (sounds like
   "accept")
   *I like every dish
   except the last one.*
ex•cep•tion
ex•cep•tion•al
ex•cerpt (v.)
ex•cerpt (n.)
ex•cess
   also pronounced
   ex•cess
ex•ces•sive
ex•change
ex•chang•ing
ex•cite
ex•cite•ment
ex•cit•ing
ex•claim

ex•cla•**ma**•tion
ex•**clude**
ex•**clud**•ing
ex•**clu**•sion
ex•**clu**•sive
ex•**crete**
ex•**cru**•ci•at•ing
ex•**cur**•sion
ex•**cuse**
ex•**cus**•ing
ex•e•cute
ex•e•cut•ing
ex•e•**cu**•tion
ex•**ec**•u•tive
ex•**empt**
ex•er•cise
ex•er•cis•ing
ex•hal•**a**•tion
ex•**hale**
ex•**hal**•ing
ex•**haust**
ex•**haus**•ting
ex•**hib**•it
ex•hi•**bi**•tion
ex•**hil**•a•rat•ing
ex•ile
ex•**ist**
ex•**ist**•ence
ex•it
ex•o•dus
ex•**on**•er•ate
ex•**or**•bi•tant
ex•or•cise
ex•or•cism

ex•o•**skel**•e•ton
ex•**ot**•ic
ex•**pand**
ex•**panse**
ex•**pect**
ex•pec•**ta**•tion
ex•pe•dite
ex•pe•dit•ing
ex•pe•**di**•tion
ex•**pel**
ex•**pelled**
ex•**pense**
ex•**pen**•sive
ex•**pe**•ri•ence
ex•**per**•i•ment
ex•**per**•i•**men**•tal
ex•pert
ex•pi•**ra**•tion
ex•**pire**
ex•**pir**•ing

exhaust

ex•**plain**
ex•**plan**•**a**•tion
ex•**plic**•it
ex•**plode**
ex•**plod**•ing
ex•ploit (n.)
ex•**ploit** (v.)
ex•plo•**ra**•tion
ex•**plore**
ex•**plor**•er
ex•**plor**•ing
ex•**plo**•sion
ex•**plo**•sive
ex•**po**•nent
ex•port (n.)
ex•**port** (v.)
 also pronounced
 ex•port
ex•por•**ta**•tion
ex•**pose**
ex•**pos**•ing
ex•**po**•sure
ex•**press**
ex•**pres**•sion
ex•**pres**•sive
ex•**press**•way
ex•**qui**•site
ex•**tend**
ex•**ten**•sion
ex•**ten**•sive
ex•**tent**
ex•**te**•ri•or
ex•**ter**•mi•nate
ex•**ter**•nal

ex•**tinct**
ex•**tinc**•tion
ex•**tin**•guish
ex•tra
ex•tract (n.)
ex•**tract** (v.)
ex•**traor**•di•nar•y

ex•tra•ter•**res**•tri•al
ex•**trav**•a•gance
ex•**trav**•a•gant
ex•**treme**
ex•tro•vert
ex•**u**•ber•ant
eye

eye•ball
eye•brow
eye•lash
eye•lid
eye•sight
eye•tooth
eye•**wit**•ness

fa·ble
fab·ric
fab·ri·cate
fab·ri·ca·tion
fab·u·lous
fa·cade
face
fa·cil·i·tate
fa·cil·i·tat·ing
fa·cil·i·ties
fa·cil·i·ty
fac·sim·i·le
fact
fac·tor
fac·to·ries
fac·to·ry
fac·tu·al
fac·ul·ties
fac·ul·ty
fad
fade
fad·ing
Fahr·en·heit
fail
fail·ure
faint (sounds like
   "feint")
   We barely heard the
   faint sound.
fair
fair·ground
fair·ies

fair·ly
fair·ness
fair·y
faith
faith·ful
faith·ful·ly
fake
fak·ing
fa·la·fel
fal·con
fall
fall·out
false
false·hood
fal·ter
fame
fa·mil·iar
fa·mil·iar·i·ty
fam·i·lies
fam·i·ly
fam·ine
fam·ished
fa·mous
fan
fa·nat·ic
fan·ci·er
fan·ci·est
fan·ci·ness
fan·cy
fang
fan·ta·sies
fan·ta·size

fan·ta·siz·ing
fan·tas·tic
fan·ta·sy
fan·zine
far
far·a·way
farce
fare
fare·well
far-fetched
farm
far·sight·ed
far·ther
fas·ci·nate
fas·ci·nat·ing
fas·ci·na·tion
fas·cism
fas·cist
fash·ion
fash·ion·a·ble
fast
fas·ten
fas·ten·er
fas·tid·i·ous
fat
fa·tal
fa·tal·i·ties
fa·tal·i·ty
fate
fate·ful
fa·ther
fath·om

fa•**tigue**
fat•ter
fat•test
fau•cet
fault
fau•na
fa•vor
fa•vor•a•ble
fa•vor•ite
fa•vor•it•ism
fawn
fax
fear
fear•ful
fear•less
fea•si•ble
feast
feat
feath•er
fea•ture
Feb•ru•ar•y
fed
fed•er•al
fed•er•**a**•tion
fee
fee•ble
feed
feed•back
feel
feet
feign
feint (sounds like "faint")

The troops made a

feint on one side of the island before actually attacking the other side.

feist•y
fe•line

feline

fell
fel•low
felt
fe•male
fem•i•nine
fem•i•nist
fence
fenc•ing
fend
fend•er
fer•**ment**
fern
fe•**ro**•cious
fe•**roc**•i•ty

fer•ret
Fer•ris **wheel**
fer•ry
fer•tile
fer•ti•li•**za**•tion
fer•ti•lize
fer•ti•liz•er
fer•ti•liz•ing
fer•vent
fes•ti•val
fes•tive
fes•**tiv**•ity
fetch
fetch•ing
fet•tuc•**ci**•ne
fe•tus
feud
feu•dal•ism
fe•ver
few
fez
fi•an•**cé** (sounds like "fi•an•cée")

Her fiancé is Mr. Jones.

fi•an•**cée** (sounds like "fi•an•cé")

He gave his fiancée a ring.

fib
fibbed
fib•bing
fi•ber
fi•ber•glass

fick•le
fic•tion
fid•dle
fid•dler
fid•dling
fidg•et
field
field•er
fiend
fierce
fier•y
fi•es•ta
fifth
fig
fight
fig•ure
fil•a•ment
file
fill
fil•let
  also pronounced
  fil•**let**
fil•ling
fil•ly
film
fil•ter
filth
fil•**tra**•tion
fin
fi•nal
fi•**na**•le
fi•nal•ist
fi•nal•ize
fi•nal•ly

fi•nance
fi•**nan**•cial
fi•**nanc**•ing
finch
find
find•ing
fine
fin•er
fin•est
fin•ger
fin•ger•nail
fin•ger•print
fin•ick•y
fin•ish
fi•nite
Fin•land
Fin•nish
fir
fire
fire•arm
fire•crack•er
fire ex•**tin**•guish•er

fire•fight•er
fire•flies
fire•fly
fire•house
fire•man
fire•place
fire•proof
fire•side
fire•trap
fire•wood
fire•works
firm
first
first•hand
first-rate
fish
fish•er•man
fish•er•y
fish•ing rod
fish•y
fis•sion
fist
fit
fit•ness
fit•ting
five
fix
fix•**a**•tion
fix•ture
fizz
fiz•zle
fjord (*or* **fiord**)
flab
flab•ber•gast•ed

flag
flag•pole
flair
flak
flake
flam•**boy**•ant
flame
fla•**min**•go
fla•**min**•gos (*or* fla•**min**•goes)
flam•ma•ble
flank
flan•nel
flap
flap•jack
flare
flash
flash•back
flash•light
flash•y
flask
flat
flat•bed
flat•car
flat•ter
flaunt (sometimes confused with "flout")
She shouldn't flaunt her A+ test score.
fla•vor
flaw
flax
flea
fleck

fledg•ling
flee
fleece
fleet
fleet•ing
Flem•ish
flesh
flew
flex
flex•i•ble
flex•time
flick
flick•er
flight
flim•sy
flinch
fling
flint
flip
flip•pant
flip•per
flirt
float
flock
flog
flood
flood•light
floor
flop
flop•py
flo•ra
flo•ral
Flor•i•da

flo•rist
floss
flot•sam
floun•der
flour
flour•ish
flout (sometimes confused with "flaunt")
To flout the dress code, come barefoot to class.
flow
flow•chart
flow•er
flu
fluc•tu•ate
flu•en•cy
flu•ent
fluff
fluff•y
flu•id
fluke
fluo•**res**•cent
fluor•i•date
fluor•i•dat•ing
fluor•i•**da**•tion
fluor•ide
fluo•rine
flur•ry
flush
flushed
flus•ter
flute

flut•ter
fly
fly•catch•er
foal
foam
fo•cus
fod•der
foe
fog
fog•horn
foil
fold
fold•er
fo•li•age
folk
folk•lore
folk•tale
fol•lies
fol•low
fol•low•ing
fol•ly
fond
fon•dle
font
food
food proc•es•sor
fool
fool•ish
fool•proof
foot
foot•ball
foot•hill
foot•ing

foot•lights
foot•note
foot•print
foot•step
for
for•age
for•**bid**
for•**bid**•den
for•**bid**•ding
force
for•ceps
forc•ing
ford
fore•cast
fore•fa•ther
fore•fin•ger
fore•ground
fore•head
for•eign
fore•most
fo•**ren**•sic
fore•run•ner
fore•**see**
fore•sight
for•est
for•est **rang**•er
for•**ev**•er
fore•word
for•feit
for•**gave**
forge
forg•er
for•ger•y

for•**get**
for•**get**•ful
for•**get**•ting
for•**give**
for•**giv**•en
for•**give**•ness
for•**giv**•ing
for•**got**
for•**got**•ten
fork
fork•lift
for•**lorn**
form
for•mal
for•**mal**•i•ty
for•**mal**•ly (often
   confused with
   "formerly")
   *Please dress
   formally.*
for•mat
for•**ma**•tion
for•mer
for•mer•ly (often
   confused with
   "formally")
   *He formerly lived
   in Spain.*
for•mi•da•ble
form•less
for•mu•la
for•**sake**
for•**sak**•en
for•**sak**•ing

fort (sounds like "forte")
The old fort still had cannons.

forte (sounds like "fort"; also pronounced **for•**te)
Her forte is tennis.

forth

forth•com•ing

for•ti•fi•**ca•**tion

for•ti•fied

for•ti•fies

for•ti•fy

fort•night

for•tress

for•tu•nate

for•tu•nate•ly

for•tune

fo•rum

for•ward

fos•sil

fos•ter

fought

foul (sounds like "fowl")
That ball was foul.

found

foun•**da•**tion

found•ry

foun•tain

four

fourth

fowl (sounds like "foul")
A pheasant is a fowl.

fox

fox•es

foy•er

frac•tal

frac•tion

frac•ture

frag•ile

frag•ment

fra•grance

fra•grant

frail

frame

frame•work

fran•chise

frank

frank•fur•ter

(**frankfurter**)

fran•tic

fraud

fray

freak

freck•le

free

free•dom

free•lance

free-range

free•way

freeze

freeze-dried

free•zer

freez•ing

freight

freight•er

French

French fries

French horn

fren•zied

fren•zy

fre•quen•cies

fre•quen•cy

fre•quent

fres•co

fres•coes (*or* **fres•**cos)

fresh

fresh•man

fresh•wa•ter

fret

fric•tion

Fri•day

fridge

fried

friend
friend•li•ness
friend•ly
friend•ship
fright
fright•en
fright•ful
frig•id
frill
fringe
Fris•bee
frisk
frisk•y
frit•**ta**•ta
frit•ter
friv•o•lous
frog
frol•ic
from
front
fron•tier
frost
frost•bite
frost•ing
frost•y
froth
frown
froze
fro•zen
fru•gal
fruit
fruit•ful

fruit•less
frus•trate
fry
fry•ing
fudge
fu•el

frog

fu•gi•tive
ful•crum
ful•**fill**
full
fum•ble
fume
fun
func•tion
func•tion•al
fund
fun•da•**men**•tal
fu•ner•al

fun•gus
fun•nel
fun•ni•er
fun•ni•est
fun•ny
fur
fu•ri•ous
fur•lough
fur•nace
fur•nish
fur•ni•ture
fur•ry
fur•ther
fur•ther•more
fu•ry
fuse
fu•se•lage
fu•sion
fuss
fuss•i•er
fuss•i•est
fuss•y
fu•tile
fu•**til**•i•ty
fu•ton
fu•ture
fuzz
fuzz•i•er
fuzz•i•est
fuzz•i•ness
fuzz•y

gab
gad·get
gag
gagged
gag·ging
gain
gait (sounds like "gate")
In those shoes, you walk with a clumsy gait.
ga·la
gal·ax·ies
gal·ax·y
gale
gal·lant
gall·blad·der
gal·ler·ies
gal·ler·y
gal·ley
gal·lon
gal·lop
gal·ore
gal·va·nize
gam·ble
gam·bling
game
gan·der
gang
gang·plank
gan·grene
  also pronounced
  gan·grene

gang·ster
gang·way
gap
gap·ing
ga·rage
gar·bage
gar·ble
gar·bled
gar·den
gar·den·er
gar·de·nia
gar·gle
gar·gling
gar·land
gar·lic
gar·ment
gar·net
gar·nish
gar·ter
gas
gash
gas·o·hol
gas·o·line
gasp
gate (sounds like "gait")
The goat ran through the open gate.
gate·way
gath·er
gaud·y

gauge (rhymes with "cage")
gaunt
gauze
gave
gav·el
gay
gaze
ga·zelle
ga·zet·teer
gaz·ing
gear
gear·shift
geese
Gei·ger coun·ter
gel
ge·la·ti
gel·a·tin (*or* gel·a·tine)
ge·la·to
gem
gen·der
gene
ge·ne·al·o·gy
gen·e·ral
gen·er·al·ize
gen·er·ate
gen·er·at·ing
gen·er·a·tion
gen·er·a·tor
gen·er·ic
gen·er·ous

ge•**net**•ics
ge•nie
gen•ius (often confused with "genus")
Such intelligence is a mark of genius.
gen•tile
gen•tle
gen•tle•man
gen•tle•ness
gent•ly
gen•tri•fi•**ca**•tion
gen•u•ine
ge•nus (often confused with "genius")
Wolves and dogs belong to the same genus.
ge•o•**de**•sic
ge•o•**graph**•i•cal
ge•**og**•ra•phy
ge•o•**log**•i•cal
ge•**ol**•o•gist
ge•**ol**•o•gy
ge•o•**met**•ric
ge•**om**•e•try
Geor•gia
ge•o•**ther**•mal
ge•**ra**•ni•um
ger•bil
ger•i•**at**•ric
germ

Ger•man
Ger•**man**•ic
Ger•man **mea**•sles
ger•mi•nate
ger•mi•nat•ing
ger•mi•**na**•tion
ges•ture
ges•tur•ing
get
get•a•way
Get•tys•burg
gey•ser
ghast•ly
ghet•to
ghost
ghost•ly
gi•ant
gib•ber•ish
gid•dy
gift
gig
gi•**gan**•tic
gig•gle
gild (sounds like "guild")
If you gild the frame, the picture will be set off quite nicely.
gill
gim•mick
gin
gin•ger
gin•ger•bread
gin•ger•ly

gin•gham
gi•**raffe**
gird•er
girl
girl•friend
girth
gist
give
gla•cier
glad
glade
glad•i•a•tor
glad•i•**o**•li (pl.)
glad•i•**o**•lus (sing.)
glad•ly
glam•or•ous
glam•our (*or* **glam**•or)
glance
gland
glare
glar•ing
glass
glass•es
glaze
gla•zier
glaz•ing
gleam
glee
glee•ful
glen
glide
glid•er
glid•ing
glim•mer

glimpse
glimps·ing
glint
glis·ten
glitch
glit·ter
gloat
glob·al
globe
glock·en·spiel
gloom
gloom·y
glo·ri·fi·**ca**·tion
glo·ri·fied
glo·ri·fies
glo·ri·fy
glo·ri·fy·ing
glor·i·ous
glo·ry
gloss
glos·sa·ries
glos·sa·ry
glove
glow
glow·worm
glu·cose
glue
glu·ing
glum
glut
glut·ted
glut·ting
glut·ton
gnarled

gnash
gnat
gnaw

gnaw

gnome
gnu
go
goad
goal
goal·ie
goat
goa·**tee**
gob·ble
gob·bling
gob·let
gob·lin
go-cart
God
god·dess
god·par·ent
goes
gog·gles
gold

gold·en·rod
gold·finch
gold·fish
golf
gon·do·la
gone
gong
good
good-**bye** (*or* good-**by**)
good-na·tured
good·ness
good·**night**
goods
good·**will**
goo·ey
goose
goose bumps
go·pher
gore
gorge
gor·geous
go·**ril**·la
gor·y
gos·pel
gos·sa·mer
gos·sip
got
Goth·ic
gouge
gourd
gour·**met** (rhymes with "say")
gov·ern
gov·ern·ment

gown
grab
grace
grace•ful
grade
grad•u•al
grad•u•ate
grad•u•at•ing
grad•u•**a**•tion
graf•**fi**•ti
graft
grain
gram
gram•mar
gram•**mat**•i•cal
gra•na•ries
gra•na•ry
grand
grand•child
grand•fa•ther
grand•moth•er
grand•pa•rent
grand•stand
gran•ite
gra•**no**•la
grant
gran•u•late
gran•u•lat•ing
gran•u•**la**•tion
grape
grape•fruit
grape•vine
graph

graveyard

graph•ic
graph•ics
graph•ite
grap•ple
grap•pling
grasp
grass
grass•hop•per
grass•land
grate
grate•ful
grat•i•fi•**ca**•tion
grat•i•fied
grat•i•fies
grat•i•fy
grat•i•tude
grave

grav•el
grave•stone
grave•yard
grav•i•ty
gra•vy
gray
graze
grease
great
Great Dane
great-grand•child
great-grand•pa•rent
greed
greed•y
green
green•horn
green•house
greet
gre•**nade**
grew
grey•hound
grid
grid•dle
grid•i•ron
grid•lock
grief
griev•ance
grieve
grill
grim
gri•mace
grime
grin

grind

grind·stone

grinned

grip

gris·ly (sounds like "grizzly")

Police are investigating a grisly murder.

grit

grits

griz·zly (sounds like "grisly")

A grizzly bear can be dangerous.

groan

gro·cer·ies

gro·cer·y

grog·gy

groom

groove

grope

gross

gro·**tesque**

grouch

grouch·y

ground

ground·ed

ground·hog

group

grove

grov·el

grow

growl

grown-up

growth

grub

grub·by

grudge

gru·el·ing

grue·some

gruff

grum·ble

grump·y

grunge

grunt

gua·ca·**mo**·le

guar·an·**tee**

guard

guard·i·an

guer·**ril**·la

guess

guest

gui·dance

guide

guide·book

guid·ing

guild (sounds like "gild")

There was a guild for weavers in medieval times.

guil·lo·tine

guilt

guilt·y

guin·ea **pig**

gui·**tar**

gulch

gulf

gull

gul·li·ble

gul·ly

gulp

gum

gum·drop

gun

gun·fire

gun·pow·der

gup·pies

gup·py

gur·gle

gur·gling

gush

gust

gus·to

gut

gut·ter

guy

guz·zle

gym

gym·**na**·si·um

gym·nast

gym·**nas**·tics

Gyp·sies

Gyp·sy

gy·rate

gy·rat·ing

gy·**ra**·tion

gy·ro·scope

ha
hab•it
hab•i•tat
ha•**bit**•u•al
ha•**bit**•u•al•ly
ha•ci•**en**•da
hack
had
had•n't
hag•gard
hag•gle
hai•ku
hail
hair (sounds like "hare")
  Please comb your hair.
hair•cut
hair•do
hair•dres•ser
hair•pin
hair-rais•ing
hair•y
half
half•heart•ed
half-**mast**
half•time
half•way
hal•i•but
hall
hal•le•**lu**•jah
hal•lowed
Hal•low•**een**
  (*or* Hal•low•**e'en**)

hal•**lu**•ci•nate
hal•**lu**•ci•nat•ing
hal•lu•ci•**na**•tion
hall•way
ha•lo
halt
hal•ter
halve (sounds like "have")
  To halve something is to cut it in two.
halves
ham
ham•burg•er
ham•mer
ham•mock
ham•per
ham•ster
hand
hand•bag
hand•ball
hand•book
hand•cuffs
hand•ful
hand•i•cap
hand•i•craft
hand•ker•chief
hand•ker•chiefs
  (*or* **hand**•ker•chieves)
han•dle
han•dle•bars
hand•made

hand-me-down
hand•out
hand•rail
hand•shake
hand•some
hand•spring
hand•stand
hand•writ•ing
hand•y
hang
han•gar (sounds like "hanger")
  The airplane is in the hangar.
hang•er (sounds like "hanger")
  Put the shirt on the hanger.
hang•o•ver
hang-up
han•ker
Ha•nuk•kah (*or* **Cha**•nu•kah)
hap•**haz**•ard
hap•pen
hap•pi•er
hap•pi•est
hap•pi•ness
hap•py
hap•py-go-**luck**•y

har•**ass**
 also pronounced
 har•ass
har•bor
hard
hard-boiled
hard•en
hard•ly
hard•ship
hard•ware
hard•wood
har•dy
hare (sounds like
 "hair")
 *The tortoise beat
 the hare.*
harm
harm•ful
harm•less
har•**mon**•i•ca
har•mo•nize
har•mo•ny
har•ness
harp
har•**poon**
harp•si•chord
harsh
har•vest
har•vest•er
has
has•n't
has•sle
haste
has•ty

hat
hatch
hatch•back
hatch•er•y

(**hatchet**)

hatch•et
hate
hate•ful
haugh•ty
haul
haunt
have (sounds like
 "halve")
 I have new shoes.
ha•ven
have•n't
hav•oc
Ha•**wai**•i
hawk
hay (sounds like "hey")
 Horses eat hay.
hay•loft
hay•stack
haz•ard

haz•ard•ous
haze
ha•zel
haz•y
he
head
head•ache
head•band
head•dress
head•**first**
head•ing
head•light
head•line
head•mas•ter
head•mis•tress
head-on
head•phones
head•quar•ters
head•strong
head•way
heal
health
heap
heaped
heap•ing
hear
heard (sounds like
 "herd")
 *I heard him say
 we won.*
hear•say
hearse
heart
heart at•**tack**

heart•beat

heart•bro•ken

hearth

heart•less

heart•y

heat

heat•er

heave

heav•en

heav•en•ly

heav•y

He•brew

heck•le

hec•tic

he'd (sounds like "heed")

He'd like that.

hedge

heed (sounds like "he'd")

Heed my warning.

heel

hef•ty

heif•er

height

height•en

Heim•lich ma•**neu**•ver

heir (sounds like "air")

She is his only heir.

heir•ess

heir•loom

hel•i•cop•ter

he•li•um

hel•**lo**

hel•met

help

help•ful

help•ing

help•less

hem

hem•i•sphere

hem•lock

he•mo•**phil**•i•a

he•mo•**phil**•i•ac

hem•or•rhage

hen

her

herb

her•bi•vore

herd (sounds like "heard")

There's a herd of cows.

here

he•**red**•i•tar•y

he•**red**•i•ty

(**helicopter**)

here's

her•i•tage

her•mit

he•ro

he•roes

he•**ro**•ic

her•o•in (sounds like "heroine")

She almost died from a heroin overdose.

her•o•ine (sounds like "heroin")

The heroine saved many lives.

her•on

her•ring

hers

her•**self**

hertz (sounds like "hurts")

A hertz is a unit of measurement.

hes•i•tate

hes•i•tat•ing

hes•i•**ta**•tion

hex•a•gon

hey (sounds like "hay")

Hey, how're you?

hi (sounds like "high")

Hi, there!

hi•ber•nate

hi•ber•**na**•tion

hic•cup

hick•o•ry

hid
hide
hide-and-**seek**
hid•e•ous
hide•out
hi•er•o•**glyph**•ics
high (sounds like "hi")

The airplane is high in the sky.

higher (sounds like "hire")

Jump higher!

high•light
high-rise
high tech (n.)
high-tech (adj.)
high•way
hi•jack
hike
hi•**lar**•i•ous
hill
hill•side
hill•top
him (sounds like "hymn")

Please give him the package.

him•**self**
hind
hin•der
Hin•du•ism
hinge
hint
hip

hip-hop
hip•pie
Hip•**poc**•ra•tes
hip•po•**pot**•a•mus
hire (sounds like "higher")

I hope they hire you for the job.

Hir•o•**shi**•ma
also pronouned
Hi•**ro**•shi•ma
his
His•**pan**•ic
hiss
his•**tor**•ic
his•**tor**•ic•al
his•to•ries
his•to•ry
hit
hitch
hitch•hike
hit•ting
hive
hoard
hoarse (sounds like "horse")

I'm too hoarse to talk.

hoax
hob•by
hock•ey
hoe
hoes (sounds like "hose")

There are two hoes in the garden shed.

hog
ho•gan
hoist
hold
hold•up
hole (sounds like "whole")

Dig a hole and plant the seeds.

hol•i•day
ho•**lis**•tic
hol•low
hol•ly
ho•lo•caust
ho•lo•gram
hol•ster
ho•ly (sounds like "wholly")

The holy man spoke words of wisdom.

Ho•ly Com•**mun**•ion
home
home•less
home•ly
home•**made**
home•mak•er
ho•me•**op**•a•thy
home•room
home run
home•sick
home•spun
home•stead
home•work

ho•**mog**•e•nize
hom•o•graph
hom•o•nym
hom•o•phone
hon•est
hon•est•ly
hon•ey
hon•ey•bee
hon•ey•comb
hon•ey•moon
hon•ey•suck•le
honk
hon•or
hon•or•able
hon•or•ably
hon•or•ar•y
hood
hoof
hook
hooked
hoop
hoo•**ray** (*or* hur•**ray**)
hoot
hop
hope
hoped
hope•ful
hope•ful•ly
hope•less
hope•less•ly
Ho•pi
hop•ing
hop•scotch

ho•**ri**•zon
hor•i•**zon**•tal
hor•mone
horn
hor•net
hor•o•scope
hor•ri•ble
hor•rid
hor•**rif**•ic
hor•ri•fy
hor•ror
horse (sounds like
　"hoarse")
　My horse loves to
　gallop.
horse•back
horse•fly
horse•play
horse•pow•er
horse•shoe
hose (sounds like
　"hoes")
　Use this hose to water
　the garden.
ho•sier•y
hos•pice
hos•pi•tal
hos•pi•**tal**•i•ty
host
hos•tage
hos•tel (sounds like
　"hostile")
　We stayed in a youth
　hostel on our trip.

host•ess
hos•tile (sounds like
　"hostel")
　Hostile people can be
　frightening.
hos•**til**•i•ty
hot
hot dog
ho•**tel**
hot-wa•ter **bot**•tle
hound
hour
hour•glass
house
house•boat
house•fly
house•hold
house•work
hous•ing
hov•er
hov•er•craft
how
how•**ev**•er
howl
hub
hud•dle
hue
huff
hug
huge
hugged
hugging
hulk

hull
hum
hu•man
hu•mane
hu•man•i•**tar**•i•an
hu•**man**•i•ty
hum•ble
hum•drum
hu•mid
hu•**mil**•i•ate
hu•mil•i•**a**•tion
hu•**mil**•i•ty
hummed
hum•ming
hum•ming•bird
hu•mor
hu•mor•ous
hump
hump•back
hunch
hunch•back
hun•dred
hun•dredth
hun•gri•er
hun•gri•est
hun•gry
hunk
hunt
hunt•er
hur•dle
hurl
hur•**rah**

hur•**ray** (*or* hoo•**ray**)
hur•ri•cane
hur•ried
hur•ries
hur•ry
hur•ry•ing
hurt
hurts (sounds like "hertz")

Getting a needle sometimes hurts.

hus•band
hush
husk
husk•y

husky

hus•tle
hus•tling
hut
hy•a•cinth
hy•brid
hy•drant
hy•dro•e•**lec**•tric
hy•dro•e•lec•**tric**•i•ty
hy•dro•foil
hy•dro•gen
hy•dro•**pon**•ics
hy•**e**•na
hy•giene
hy•**gien**•ist
hymn (sounds like "him")

We sang a hymn in church.

hym•nal
hype
hy•per•**ac**•tive
hy•phen
hyp•no•tize
hy•po•**chon**•dri•ac
hyp•o•crite
hy•po•**der**•mic
hy•**pot**•e•nuse
hy•po•**ther**•mi•a
hy•**poth**•e•sis
hys•**ter**•i•a
hys•**ter**•i•cal

ice
ice•berg
ice•cap
ice cream
Ice•land
ice-skate (v.)
ice skate (n.)
i•ci•cle
ic•ing
i•con
i•cy
I'd
I•da•ho
i•**de**•a
i•**de**•al
i•**den**•ti•cal
i•den•ti•fi•**ca**•tion
i•**den**•ti•fy
id•i•om
id•i•ot
i•dle (sounds like "idol")

The idle man didn't want to work.

i•dol (sounds like "idle")

The movie star is her idol.

if
ig•loo
ig•ne•ous
ig•**nite**

ig•**ni**•tion
ig•no•rance
ig•no•rant
ig•**nore**
i•**gua**•na
ill
I'll (sounds like "aisle" and "isle")

I'll see you tomorrow.

il•**le**•gal
il•**le**•gal•ly
il•**leg**•i•ble
Il•li•**nois**
il•**lit**•er•a•cy
il•**lit**•er•ate
il•**log**•i•cal
il•**lu**•mi•nate
il•lu•mi•**na**•tion

igloo

il•**lu**•sion
il•lus•trate
il•lus•**tra**•tion
I'm
im•age
im•age•ry
i•**mag**•i•nar•y
i•mag•i•**na**•tion
i•**mag**•i•na•tive
im•**ag**•ine
im•i•tate
im•i•tat•ing
im•i•**ta**•tion
im•**mac**•u•late
im•ma•**ture**
im•**mea**•sur•a•ble
im•**me**•di•ate
im•**me**•di•ate•ly
im•**mense**
im•**men**•si•ty
im•**merse**
im•**mer**•sion
im•mi•grant
im•mi•**gra**•tion
im•**mo**•bi•lize
im•**mor**•al
im•**mor**•tal
im•**mune**
im•**mune sys**•tem
im•**mu**•ni•ty
im•mu•ni•**za**•tion
im•mu•nize

im•pact

im•**pair**

im•**par**•tial

im•**pa**•tient

im•**peach**

im•**peach**•ment

im•**per**•a•tive

im•**per**•fect

im•**pe**•ri•al

im•**per**•son•al

im•**per**•son•ate

im•**plant** (v.)

im•plant (n.)

im•ple•ment

im•po•**lite**

im•port (n.)

im•**port** (v.)
  also pronounced
  im•port

im•**por**•tance

im•**por**•tant

im•pos•si•**bil**•i•ty

im•**pos**•si•ble

im•**pos**•tor

im•**prac**•ti•cal

im•**press**

im•**pres**•sion

im•**pres**•sive

im•print (n.)

im•print (v.)

im•**prop**•er

im•**prove**

im•**prove**•ment

im•pro•vi•**sa**•tion

im•pro•vise

im•pu•dent

im•pulse

im•**pul**•sive

im•**pu**•ri•ty

in (sounds like"inn")
  The bird is in the nest.

in•**ac**•cu•ra•cy

in•**ac**•cu•rate

in•**ad**•e•quate

in•ap•**pro**•pri•ate

in•ar•**tic**•u•late

in•**au**•di•ble

in•**au**•gu•rate

in•au•gu•**ra**•tion

in•can•**des**•cent

in•**ca**•pa•ble

in•cense

in•**cen**•tive

in•**ces**•sant

inch

inch•worm

in•ci•dent

in•ci•**den**•tal•ly

in•**cin**•er•ate

in•**cin**•er•a•tor

in•**ci**•sion

in•cli•**na**•tion

in•**cline** (v.)

in•cline (n.)

in•**clined**

in•**clude**

in•**clu**•sion

in•co•**her**•ent

in•come

in•com•**pat**•i•ble

in•**com**•pe•tent

in•com•**plete**

in•com•pre•**hen**•si•ble

in•con•**ceiv**•a•ble

in•con•**clu**•sive

in•con•**sid**•er•ate

in•con•**spic**•u•ous

in•con•**ven**•ience

in•con•**ven**•ient

in•**cor**•por•ate

in•cor•**rect**

in•**crease** (v.)

in•crease (n.)

in•**cred**•i•ble

in•**crim**•i•nate

in•cu•bate

in•cu•ba•tor

in•**cur**•a•ble

in•**debt**•ed

in•**deed**

in•**dent**

in•de•**pen**•dence

in•de•**pen**•dent

in•de•**struc**•ti•ble

in•dex

In•di•an

In•di•**an**•a

in•di•cate

in•di•**ca**•tion

in•**dif**•fer•ent

in•di•**ges**•tion

in•**dig**•nant

in•di•go
in•di•**rect**
in•dis•**pen**•sa•ble
in•di•**vid**•u•al
in•di•vid•u•**al**•i•ty
in•di•**vis**•i•ble
in•door
in•**doors**
in•**dulge**
in•**dus**•tri•al
in•**dus**•tri•al•ize
in•dus•tries
in•dus•try
in•ef•**fi**•cien•cy
in•ef•**fi**•cient
in•e•**qual**•i•ty
in•**ert**
in•**er**•tia
in•**ev**•i•ta•ble
in•ex•**pen**•sive
in•ex•**pe**•ri•enced
in•fa•mous
in•fant
in•fan•try
in•**fat**•u•at•ed
in•fat•u•**a**•tion
in•**fect**
in•**fec**•tion
in•**fec**•tious
in•**fer**
in•fer•ence
in•**fe**•ri•or
in•fer•**til**•i•ty
in•**fes**•ted

in•**fil**•trate
in•fil•**tra**•tion
in•fi•nite
in•**fin**•i•tive
in•**fin**•i•ty
in•**firm**
in•**fir**•ma•ry
in•**flame**
in•**flam**•ma•ble
in•flam•**ma**•tion
in•**flat**•a•ble
in•**flate**
in•**fla**•tion
in•**flex**•i•ble
in•**flict**
in•flu•ence
in•flu•**en**•tial
in•flu•**en**•za
in•fo•**mer**•cial
in•**form**
in•**for**•mal
in•**for**•mal•ly
in•for•**ma**•tion
in•for•**ma**•tion•al
in•**for**•ma•tive
in•**fre**•quent
in•**fu**•ri•ate
in•**fu**•ri•at•ing
in•**gre**•di•ent
in•**ha**•bit
in•ha•**la**•tion
in•**hale**
in•**hal**•er
in•**her**•it

in•**her**•it•ance
in•**hib**•it
in•**hu**•man
in•**i**•tial
i•**ni**•ti•ate
in•i•ti•**a**•tion
in•**i**•tia•tive
in•**ject**
in•jure
in•**ju**•ry
in•**jus**•tice
ink
in•land
in•let
in•mate
inn (sounds like "in")
   We stayed at a
   country inn.
in•ner
in•ning
in•no•cence
in•no•cent
in•no•**va**•tion
in•nu•mer•ate
in•**oc**•u•late
in•pa•tient
in•put
in•**quire**
in•**quir**•y
   also pronounced
   in•quir•y
in•**quis**•i•tive
in•sane
in•**scribe**

in·**scrip**·tion
in·sect
in·**sec**·ti·cide
in·se·**cure**
in·**sen**·si·tive
in·sen·si·**tiv**·i·ty
in·**sert** (v.)
in·sert (n.)
in·**side**
  also pronounced
  in·side
in·sight
in·**sig**·ni·a
in·sig·**nif**·i·cant
in·sin·**cere**
in·**sist**
in·**sis**·tence
in·**sis**·tent
in·**sol**·u·ble
in·**som**·ni·a
in·**spect**
in·**spec**·tion
in·**spec**·tor
in·**spire**
in·**stall**
in·**stall**·ment
in·stance
in·stant
in·**stead**
in·**still**
in·stinct
in·sti·tute
in·sti·**tu**·tion
in·sti·**tu**·tion·al

in·**struct**
in·**struc**·tion
in·stru·ment

instrument

in·suf·**fi**·cient
in·su·late
in·su·lin
in·**sult** (v.)
in·sult (n.)
in·**sur**·ance
in·**sure**
in·te·ger
in·te·grate
in·te·**gra**·tion
in·**teg**·rity
in·tel·lect
in·tel·**lec**·tu·al
in·**tel**·li·gence
in·**tel**·li·gent
in·**tel**·li·gi·ble
in·**tend**
in·**tense**

in·**ten**·si·fy
in·**tent**
in·**ten**·tion
in·ter·**ac**·tive
in·ter·**cept**
in·ter·**change**·a·ble
in·ter·com
in·ter·est
in·ter·face
in·ter·**fere**
in·ter·**fer**·ence
in·ter·ga·**lac**·tic
in·**te**·ri·or
in·ter·**jec**·tion
in·ter·**me**·di·ate
in·ter·**mis**·sion
in·ter·**mit**·tent
in·tern
in·**ter**·nal
in·ter·**na**·tion·al
In·ter·net
in·ter·**plan**·e·tar·y
in·**ter**·pret
in·ter·pre·**ta**·tion
in·**ter**·ro·gate
in·ter·**rupt**
in·ter·**sect**
in·ter·**sec**·tion
  also pronounced
  in·ter·sec·tion
in·ter·**state**
in·ter·val
in·ter·**vene**
in·ter·view

in•**tes**•tine
in•ti•mate
in•**tim**•i•date
in•tim•i•**da**•tion
in•to
in•**tol**•er•a•ble
in•**tol**•er•ance
in•**tol**•er•ant
in•**tox**•i•ca•ted
in•**tran**•si•tive
in•tri•cate
in•trigue
in•tro•**duce**
in•tro•**duc**•tion
in•tro•**duc**•to•ry
in•tro•vert
in•**trude**
in•tu•**i**•tion
In•u•it
in•**vade**
in•va•lid (n.)
in•**val**•id (adj.)
in•**val**•u•a•ble
in•**var**•i•a•bly
in•**vent**
in•**ven**•tion
in•ven•to•ry
in•**vert**
in•**ver**•te•brate
in•**vest**
in•**ves**•ti•gate

in•**vin**•ci•ble
in•**vis**•i•ble
in•vi•**ta**•tion
in•**vite**
in•**volve**
in•**volved**
in•ward
i•o•dine
i•on
I•o•wa
i•rate
  also pronounced
  i•**rate**
i•ris
I•rish
i•ron
i•**ron**•ic
i•ro•ny
I•ro•quois
ir•**ra**•tio•nal
ir•**reg**•u•lar
ir•**rel**•e•vance
ir•**rel**•e•vant
ir•re•**sist**•i•ble
ir•re•**spon**•si•ble
ir•re•**vers**•i•ble
ir•ri•gate
ir•ri•**ga**•tion
ir•ri•ta•ble
ir•ri•tate
ir•ri•**ta**•tion

Is•lam
Is•**lam**•ic
is•land
isle (sounds like "aisle"
  and "I'll")
  We went to a small,
  sunny isle for our
  vacation.
is•n't
i•so•late
i•so•**met**•rics
i•**sos**•ce•les
is•sue
isth•mus
it
i•**tal**•ic
itch
i•tem
i•tem•ize
i•**tin**•er•ar•y
its (sounds like "it's")
  The dog buried its
  bone.
it's (sounds like "its")
  It's time to go.
it•**self**
I've
i•vo•ry
i•vy

jab
jabbed
jab•bing
jack
jack•et
jack•ham•mer
jack•knife
jack-o'-lan•tern
jack•pot
jack•rab•bit
Ja•**cuz**•zi
jade
jag•ged
jag•uar
jail
jail•bird
jam
jam•bor•**ee**
jan•i•tor
Jan•u•ar•y
Ja•**pan**
Jap•a•**nese**
jar
jar•gon
jave•lin
jaw
jay•walk
jazz
jeal•ous
jeans
jeep
jeer

Je•**ho**•vah
Jell-O
jel•ly
jel•ly•fish
jeop•ar•dize
jeop•ard•y
jerk
jest
jest•er

jester

Je•sus
jet
jet•ti•son
jet•ty
Jew
jew•el

jew•el•er
jew•el•ry
Jew•ish
jif•fy
jig
jig•saw
jin•gle
jinx
job
jock•ey
jog
jogged
jog•ger
jog•ging
join
join•er
joint
joke
jol•ly
jolt
jon•quil
jour•nal
jour•na•lism
jour•nal•ist
jour•ney
joust
jo•vi•al
jowl
joy
joy•ful
joy•ous
joy•stick

ju•bi•lant
ju•bi•**la**•tion
ju•bi•lee
Ju•da•ism
judge
judg•ment (*or*
  judge•ment)
ju•**di**•cial
ju•**di**•cious
ju•do
jug
jug•gle

juice
juke•box
Ju•**ly**
jum•ble
jum•bo
jump
jum•per
junc•tion
June
jun•gle
jun•ior
junk

junk•yard
Ju•pi•ter
ju•ror
ju•ry
just
jus•tice
jus•ti•fi•**ca**•tion
jus•ti•fied
jus•ti•fies
jus•ti•fy
ju•ve•nile
jux•ta•**pose**

K

ka•**bob** (or ke•**bob**)
ka•**lei**•do•scope
kan•ga•**roo**
Kan•sas
kar•a•**o**•ke
kar•at (sounds like
  "carat," "caret," and
  "carrot")
  *This bracelet is made
  of 14-karat gold.*
ka•**ra**•te
kay•ak
ke•**bob** (or ka•**bob**)
keen
keep
keep•er
keep•sake
kelp
ken•nel
Ken•**tuck**•y
kept
ker•chief
ker•chiefs (or
  ker•chieves)
ker•nel
ker•o•sene
ketch•up
ket•tle
ket•tle•drum
key (sounds like
  "quay")
  *Here is the key to the
  door.*

key•board
key•hole
key•pad
kha•ki
kib•**butz**
kick

(**kitten**)

kick•off
kid
kid•ded
kid•ding
kid•nap
kid•nap•per
kid•nap•ping
kid•ney
kill
kiln
ki•lo•gram
ki•**lo**•meter
ki•lo•watt
kilt

ki•**mo**•no
kin
kind
kin•der•gar•ten
kind•heart•ed
kind•ness
ki•**net**•ic
king
king•dom
kink
kin•ship
ki•osk
kiss
kit
kitch•en
kite
kit•ten
kit•ty
ki•wi
klep•to•**ma**•ni•ac
klutz
knack
knap•sack
knave
knead (sounds like
  "need")
  *Please knead the
  dough.*
knee
kneel
knew
knick•ers

knife

knight (sounds like "night")

A knight slew the dragon.

knight•hood

knit (sounds like "nit")

I'll knit a sweater for Grandma.

knit•ted

knit•ting

knives

knob

knock

knock•er

knoll

knot (sounds like "not")

He tied a square knot.

knot•ty

know (sounds like "no")

I know the name of the secret guest.

know-how

know•ledge

known

knuck•le

ko•**a**•la

kook

Ko•**ran** (or Qur'•**an**)

Ko•**re**•a

kos•her

Krem•lin

kryp•ton

kum•quat

kung fu

Kwan•za (or **Kwan**•zaa)

L

lab
la•bel
la•beled
la•bor
lab•o•ra•tor•ies
lab•o•ra•tor•y
lace
lac•ing
lack
lacks (sounds like
  "lax")
  *This sauce lacks
  flavor.*
lack•a•**dai**•si•cal
lack•lus•ter
lac•quer
la•**crosse**
lad
lad•der

ladder

la•dies
la•dle
la•dy
la•dy•bug
lag
lagged
lag•ging
la•**goon**
laid-back
lake
lamb
lame
lamp
lance
lanc•ing
land
land•fill
land•ing
land•la•dies
land•la•dy
land•lord
land•mark
land•scape
land•slide
lane
lan•guage
lank•y
lan•tern
lan•yard
lap
la•**pel**
Lap•land

lap•top
lard
large
large•ly
la•ri•at
lark
lar•va (sing.)
lar•vae (pl.)
lar•yn•**gi**•tis
lar•ynx
la•**sa**•gna (or
  la•**sa**•gne)
la•ser
lash
lass
las•so
  also pronounced
  las•**so**
las•sos (or las•soes)
last
last•ing
latch
latch•key
late
late•com•er
late•ly
lat•er•al
la•tex
lathe
lath•er
Lat•in
La•**ti**•na

Lat•in
A•**mer**•i•can
La•**ti**•no
lat•i•tude
laugh
laugh•a•ble
laugh•ter
launch
laun•der
laun•dries
laun•dry
lau•rel
la•va
lav•a•tory
lav•en•der
lav•ish
law
law-a•**bid**•ing
law•ful
lawn
lawn•mow•er
law•suit
law•yer
lax (sounds like "lacks")

The teacher was lax in collecting homework.

lay (sounds like "lei")

Did the hen lay this egg?

lay•er
lay•off
lay•out
la•zi•er

la•zi•est
la•zi•ness
la•zy
lead (rhymes with "bead")

The guide will lead us out of the jungle.

lead (rhymes with "bed")

Lead is a heavy metal.

lead•er•**ship**
leaf
leaf•let
league
leak (sounds like "leek")

The plumber fixed the leak.

lawnmower

lean
lean•ing
leap
leap•frog

learn
learned
learn•ing
lease
leash
least
leath•er
leave
leaves
leav•ing
Leb•a•non
lec•ture
ledge
leech
leek (sounds like "leak")

A leek is related to an onion.

left
left-**hand**•ed
left•overs
leg
leg•a•cies
leg•a•cy
le•gal
leg•end
leg•gings
leg•i•ble
le•gion
leg•is•late
leg•is•**la**•tion
leg•is•la•tor
leg•is•la•ture
le•**git**•i•mate

lei (sounds like "lay")
The girl wore a lei of orchids around her neck.

leis•ure

lei•sure•ly

lem•on

lem•on•**ade**

lend

length

length•en

le•ni•ent

lens

lens•es

Lent

len•til

leop•ard

le•o•tard

less

les•sen (sounds like "lesson")
This medicine will lessen the pain.

less•ened

les•son (sounds like "lessen")
The math lesson wasn't so hard.

let

leth•al

let's

let•ter

let•ter•ing

let•ting

let•tuce

leu•**ke**•mi•a

lev•ee (sounds like "levy")
The levee holds the river back.

lev•el

lev•er

lev•i•tate

lev•y (sounds like "levee")
The council will levy a new tax.

li•a•ble

li•ar (sounds like "lyre")
She has a reputation as a liar.

lib•er•al

lib•er•al•ism

lib•er•ate

lib•er•at•ed

lib•er•at•ing

lib•er•**a**•tion

Li•**be**•ria

lib•er•ties

lib•er•ty

li•**brar**•i•an

li•brar•ies

li•brar•y

lice

li•cense

li•cens•ing

lick

lic•o•rice

lid

lie (sounds like "lye")
Lie back and relax.

lieu•**ten**•ant

life

life•boat

life•guard

life•less

life•like

life•long

life pre•**serv**•er

life•style

life•time

lift

lift•off

lig•a•ment

light

light•en

light•house

light•ning

light•weight

light-year

lik•a•ble

like

like•ly

like•ness

li•lac

lil•ies

lil•y

limb

lim•ber

lime

lime•light

lim•er•ick
lime•stone
lim•it
lim•it•ed
lim•it•less
limp
Lin•coln
line
lin•e•ar
lin•en
lin•ger
lin•**gui**•ne
lin•ing
link
li•**no**•le•um
lint
li•on
li•on•ess
lip
lip-read
lip•stick
liq•ue•fy
liq•uid
liq•uor
lisp
list
lis•ten
li•ter
lit•er•a•cy
lit•er•al•ly
lit•er•ate
lit•er•a•ture
lit•mus pa•per
lit•ter

lit•tle
liv•a•ble
live
live•li•hood
live•ly
liv•er
live•stock
liv•id
liv•ing
liz•ard
lla•ma
load
loaf
loaf•er
loam
loan (sounds like
   "lone")
   *I need a loan from
   the bank.*
loathe
loath•some
loaves
lob
lobbed
lob•bies
lob•bing
lob•by
lob•ster
lo•cal
lo•cal•ly
lo•cate
lo•cat•ed
lo•cat•ing
lo•**ca**•tion

lock
lock•er
lock•er **room**
lock•et
lock•jaw
lock•smith
lo•co•**mo**•tion
lo•co•**mo**•tive
lodge
lodg•er
loft
loft•y
log
logged
log•ging
log•ic
lo•go
loin
loi•ter
loll
lol•li•pop
lone (sounds like
   "loan")
   *She was the lone
   person on the bus.*
lone•li•ness
lone•ly
lone•some
long
long-**dis**•tance
long•hand
lon•gi•tude
long-range
long•ship

long-term
long-**win**·ded
loo·fah
look
look·ing
look·out
loon
loop
loose
loose-leaf
loos·en
loot (sounds like "lute")

The loot was hidden underneath a floorboard.

lop·sid·ed
lord
lose
lo·sing
loss
lot
lo·tion
lot·ter·ies
lot·ter·y
lo·tus
loud
loud·speak·er
Lou·i·si·**an**·a
lounge
lov·a·ble
love
love·bird
love·li·est

love·ly
low
low·er
low·er·**case**
loy·al
loy·al·ly
loy·al·ty
lu·bri·cate
luck
luck·i·ly
luck·y
lu·di·crous
lug
lug·gage
lugged

(**luggage**)

lug·ging
luke·warm
lull
lul·la·by

lum·ber
lum·ber·jack
lu·mi·nous
lump
lump·y
lu·nar
lunch
lung
lunge
lurch
lure
lur·ing
lurk
lus·cious
lush
lust
lus·ter
lute (sounds like "loot")

The lute is a musical instrument.

lux·u·ries
lux·u·ry
lye (sounds like "lie")

Be careful when you pour the lye.

Lyme dis·**ease**
lymph
lynx
lyre (sounds like "liar")

She played the lyre while he sang.

lyr·ic
lyr·i·cal
lyr·ics

M

ma'am
ma•**ca**•bre
mac•a•**ro**•ni
ma•**chet**•e
ma•**chine**
ma•**chin**•er•y
ma•**chin**•ist
mack•er•el
mad
mad•am
mag•a•zine
mag•ic
mag•i•cal
mag•i•cal•ly
ma•**gi**•cian
mag•ma
mag•**ne**•si•um
mag•net
mag•**net**•ic
mag•net•ize
mag•ni•fi•**ca**•tion
mag•**nif**•i•cence
mag•**nif**•i•cent
mag•ni•fied
mag•ni•fi•er
mag•ni•fies
mag•ni•fy
mag•ni•tude
mag•**no**•li•a
ma•**hog**•a•ny
maid
maid•en

mail (sounds like "male")
The check is in the mail.
mail•box
mail car•ri•er

mail carrier

mail•man
maim
main (sounds like "Maine" and "mane")
I don't understand the main idea.
Maine (sounds like "main" and "mane")
Delicious lobsters come from Maine.
main•frame
main•land

main•ly
main•stay
main•stream
main•**tain**
maize (sounds like "maze")
Maize is another word for corn.
ma•jes•tic
ma•**jes**•ti•cal•ly
maj•es•ties
maj•es•ty
ma•jor
ma•jor•**ette**
ma•**jor**•i•ty
make
make-be•lieve
make•shift
make•up
ma•**lar**•i•a
male (sounds like "mail")
That male bird has bright feathers.
mal•ice
ma•**li**•cious
ma•**lig**•nan•cies
ma•**lig**•nan•cy
ma•**lig**•nant
mall
mal•lard
mal•let

mal•nu•**tri**•tion

malt

malt•ed

mam•mal

mam•moth

man

man•age

man•a•ger

man•a•tee

Man•da•rin

man•date

man•do•lin

mane (sounds like "Maine" and "main")

Be sure to brush the horse's mane.

ma•**neu**•ver

man•ger

man•gle

man•go

Man•**hat**•tan

man•hole

man•hood

ma•ni•ac

man•i•cure

ma•**nip**•u•late

ma•nip•u•**la**•tion

man•kind

man-made

manned

man•ner (sounds like "manor")

They spoke in a friendly manner.

man•ning

man•or (sounds like "manner")

The duke was the lord of the manor.

man•sion

man•slaugh•ter

man•u•al

man•u•**fac**•ture

man•u•**fac**•tur•er

man•u•**fac**•tur•ing

ma•**nure**

man•u•script

man•y

map

ma•ple

mar•a•thon

mar•ble

march

March

Mar•di Gras

mare

mar•ga•rine

mar•gin

mar•i•gold

mar•i•**juan**•a

ma•**ri**•na

mar•i•**na**•ra

ma•**rine**

Ma•**rine Corps**

mar•i•o•**nette**

mar•i•time

mark

mar•ket

mar•ma•lade

ma•**roon**

ma•**rooned**

ma•**roon**•ing

mar•**quee**

mar•riage

mar•ried

mar•ries

mar•row

mar•ry

mar•ry•ing

Mars

marsh

mar•shal (sounds like "martial")

The marshal arrested the cow thief.

marsh•mal•low

mar•**su**•pi•al

mar•tial (sounds like "marshal")

During the war, martial law was declared.

Mar•tin **Lu**•ther **King,** Jr.

mar•tyr

mar•tyr•dom

mar•vel

mar•vel•ous

mar•vel•ous•ly

Mar•y•land

mas•**car**•a

mas•cot

mas•cu•line

mash

mask

ma•son

ma•son•ry

mas•quer•**ade**

mass

Mas•sa•**chu**•setts

mas•sa•cre

mas•**sage**

mas•sive

mass me•di•a

mass tran•sit

mast

mas•ter

mas•ter•mind

mas•ter•piece

mat

mat•a•dor

match

mate

ma•**te**•ri•al

ma•te•ri•al•**is**•tic

ma•**te**•ri•al•ize

ma•**ter**•nal

ma•**ter**•ni•ty

math

math•e•**mat**•i•cal

math•e•ma•**ti**•cian

math•e•**mat**•ics

mat•i•**nee**

mat•ri•mo•ny

ma•tron

matte

mat•ted

mat•ter

mat•tress

ma•**ture**

ma•**ture**•ly

ma•**tu**•ri•ty

maul

mau•so•**le**•um

mauve

max•i•mum

may

May

Ma•ya

Ma•yan

may•be

May•day

may•hem

May•flow•er

may•on•naise
    also pronounced
    may•on•**naise**

may•or

maze (sounds
    like"maize")

I got lost in the maze.

me

mead•ow

mea•ger

meal

mean

me•**an**•der

mean•ing

meant

mean•time

mean•while

mea•sles

mea•sly

meas•ure

meat (sounds like
    "meet")

*She's a meat-and-
    potatoes kid.*

me•**chan**•ic

me•**chan**•i•cal

mech•a•nism

med•al (sounds like
    "meddle")

*She won a medal
    for bravery.*

med•dle (sounds like
    "medal")

*Don't meddle in their
    friendship.*

med•dle•some

med•dling

me•di•a

me•di•an

med•ic

Med•i•caid

med•i•cal

med•i•cal•ly

Med•i•care

med•i•cine

me•di•**e**•val

me•di•**o**•cre

med•i•tate

med•i•tat•ed

med•i•tat•ing

med•i•**ta**•tion

me·di·um
med·ley
meek
meet (sounds like "meat")
I'd like you to meet my mom.
meet·ing
meg·a·byte
meg·a·phone
mel·an·**chol**·ic
mel·an·cho·ly
meld
mel·low
me·**lod**·ic
mel·o·dies
me·**lo**·di·ous
me·**lo**·di·ous·ness
mel·o·dra·ma
mel·o·dra·**mat**·ic
mel·o·dy
mel·on
melt
melt·down
mem·ber
mem·ber·ship
mem·brane
me·**men**·to
mem·o
mem·oir
mem·o·ra·**bil**·ia
mem·o·ra·ble
mem·o·**ran**·dum
me·**mo**·ri·al

mem·o·ries
mem·o·rize
mem·o·riz·ing
mem·o·ry
men
men·ace
mend
me·**no**·rah

menorah

men·tal
men·tion
men·u
me·**ow**
mer·ce·nar·ies
mer·ce·nar·y
mer·chan·dise
mer·chant
mer·cies
merc·i·ful
mer·cu·ry
Mer·cu·ry

mer·cy
mere
mere·ly
merge
merg·er
me·**rid**·i·an
mer·it
mer·maid
mer·ri·er
mer·ri·est
mer·ri·ness
mer·ry
mer·ry-go-round
me·sa
mesh
mess
mes·sage
mes·sen·ger
me·**tab**·o·lism
met·al
met·a·**mor**·pho·sis
met·a·phor
me·te·or
me·te·or·ite
me·te·o·**rol**·o·gist
me·te·or·**ol**·o·gy
me·ter
meth·ane
meth·od
me·**thod**·i·cal
me·**tic**·u·lous
met·ric
met·ro·**pol**·i·tan
mice

Mich•i•gan
mi•crobe
mi•cro•chip
mi•cro•com•pu•ter
mi•cro•**or**•gan•ism
mi•cro•phone
mi•cro•scope
mi•cro•**scop**•ic
mi•cro•wave
mid•day
mid•dle
mid•dle-**aged**
Mid•dle **Ag**•es
Mid•dle **East**
mid•get
mid•night
mid•way
Mid•**west**
mid•wife
might
mi•graine
mi•grant
mi•grate
mi•grat•ing
mi•**gra**•tion
mi•gra•to•ry
mild
mil•dew
mile
mile•stone
mil•i•tant
mil•i•tar•y
mi•**li**•tia
milk

milk•y
Milk•y **Way**
mill
mil•**len**•ni•um
mil•li•gram
mil•li•me•ter
mil•lion
mil•lion•**aire**
mime
mim•ic
mince
mince•meat
mind
mine
min•er (sounds like
"minor")

*The men all worked
as coal miners.*

miner

min•e•ral
min•gle

min•i•a•ture
min•i•mize
min•i•mum
min•i•ser•ies
min•i•skirt
min•is•ter
min•is•tered
mink
Min•ne•**so**•ta
min•now
mi•nor (sounds like
  "miner")

*Since he's a minor, he
needs his parents'
permission.*

mi•**nor**•i•ty
min•strel
mint
min•u•end
mi•nus
min•ute (n.)
min•**ute** (adj.)
min•ute•man
mir•a•cle
mi•**rage**
mir•ror
mis•be•**have**
mis•be•**hav**•ing
mis•be•**hav**•ior
mis•**cal**•cu•late
mis•cal•cu•**la**•tion
mis•**car**•riage
  also pronounced
  mis•car•riage

mis•cel•**la**•ne•ous
mis•chief
mis•**con**•duct
mi•ser
mis•er•a•ble
mis•fit
mis•**for**•tune
mis•**giv**•ing
mis•**guid**•ed
mis•hap
mis•in•**form**
mis•in•for•**ma**•tion
mis•**lay**
mis•**lead**
mis•**place**
mis•print
mis•pro•**nounce**
miss
mis•sile
mis•sing
mis•sion
mis•sion•ar•y
Mis•sis•**sip**•pi
Mis•**sou**•ri
mis•**spell**
mist
mis•**take**
mis•**tak**•en
mis•**tak**•en•ly
mis•ter
mis•tle•toe
mis•**took**
mis•**treat**
mis•**treat**•ment

mis•tress
mis•**trust**
mis•un•der•**stand**
mis•un•der•**stand**•ing
mis•un•der•**stood**
mis•**use**
mite
mitt
mit•ten
mix
mix•ture
mix-up
moan
moat
mob
mobbed
mob•bing
mo•bile
moc•ca•sin
mock
mock•ing•bird
mode
mod•el
mo•dem
mod•er•ate
mod•er•at•ing
mod•er•**a**•tion
mod•ern
mod•ern•i•**za**•tion
mod•ern•ize
mod•est
mod•es•ty
mod•i•fi•**ca**•tion
mod•i•fied

mod•i•fi•er
mod•i•fies
mod•i•fy
mod•ule
Mo•**ham**•med
  (or Mu•**ham**•mad)
Mo•hawk
moist
moist•en
moist•ure
mo•lar
mo•**las**•ses
mold
mold•y
mole
mo•**lec**•u•lar
mol•e•cule
mol•lusk
molt
mol•ten
mom
mo•ment
mo•men•**tar**•i•ly
mo•men•tar•y
mo•**men**•tum
mon•arch
mon•ar•chy
mon•as•ter•ies
mon•as•ter•y
mo•**nas**•tic
Mon•day
mon•ey
Mon•**go**•li•a
mon•i•tor

monk
mon·key
mon·key **wrench**
mon·o·**lin**·gual
mon·o·logue
mon·o·nu·cle·**o**·sis
mo·**nop**·o·lies
mo·nop·o·**lis**·tic
mo·**nop**·o·lize
mo·**nop**·o·liz·ing
mo·**nop**·o·ly
mon·o·rail
mo·**not**·o·nous
mo·**not**·o·ny
mon·**soon**
mon·ster
mon·**stros**·i·ty
mon·strous
Mon·**tan**·a
Mon·te·**zu**·ma
month
month·ly
mon·u·ment
mon·u·**men**·tal
mon·u·**men**·tal·ly
mood
mood·y
moon
moon·light
moor (sounds like "more")
Moor your boat to the dock.
moose (sounds like "mousse")
We saw a moose in the woods.
mop
mope
moped
mopped
mop·ping
mor·al
mo·**rale**
mo·**ral**·i·ty
mor·al·ly
mor·bid
more (sounds like "moor")
I want more, not less.
more·**o**·ver
Mor·mon
morn·ing (sounds like "mourning")
Every morning I watch the sunrise.
morn·ing **glo**·ry
mo·**rose**
morph
Morse code
mor·sel
mor·tal
mor·**tal**·i·ty
mor·tar
mort·gage
mor·tu·ar·y
mo·**sa**·ic
Mos·cow
Mo·ses
mosh·ing
Mos·lem (or **Mus**·lim)
mosque
mos·**qui**·to
moss
most
most·ly
mo·tel
moth
moth·er
moth·er-in-law
moth·ers-in-law
Moth·er's **Day**
mo·tion
mo·tion·less
mo·ti·vate
mo·ti·vat·ing
mo·ti·**va**·tion
mo·tive
mo·tor
mo·tor·bike
mo·tor·boat
mo·tor·cade
mo·tor·cy·cle
mo·tor·ist
mot·tled
mot·to
mound
mount
moun·tain
moun·tain·**eer**
mourn
mourn·er

mourn•ful

mourn•ing (sounds like "morning")

They are mourning his death.

mouse

mousse (sounds like "moose")

Chocolate mousse is a great dessert.

mous•tache (or mus•tache)

moustache

mous•y

mouth

mouth•piece

mov•a•ble (or move•a•ble)

move

move•ment

mov•ie

mov•ing

mow

moz•za•**rel**•la

Mr.

Mrs.

Ms.

much

muck

mu•cus

mud

mud•di•er

mud•di•est

mud•dle

mud•dy

mud•guard

muf•fin

muf•fle

muf•fler

mug

mug•gy

Mu•**ham**•mad (or Mo•**ham**•med)

mul•ber•ry

mule

mul•ti•**cul**•tur•al

mul•ti•**lin**•gual

mul•ti•**me**•di•a

mul•ti•**na**•tion•al

mul•ti•ple

mul•ti•ple scle•**ro**•sis

mul•ti•pli•**cand**

mul•ti•pli•**ca**•tion

mul•ti•plied

mul•ti•pli•er

mul•ti•plies

mul•ti•ply

mul•ti•ply•ing

mul•ti•**ra**•cial

mul•ti•tude

mum•ble

mum•mies

mum•my

mumps

munch

mun•**dane**

mu•**nic**•i•pal

mu•nic•i•**pal**•i•ty

mu•ral

mur•der

murk•i•er

murk•i•est

murk•i•ness

murk•y

mur•mur

mus•cle (sounds like "mussel")

This muscle is sore.

mus•cu•lar

muse

mu•se•um

mush

mush•room

mu•sic

mu•si•cal

mu•si•cian

musk

mus•ket

mus•ket•**eer**

musk•rat

Mus•lim (*or* **Mos**•lem)

mus•sel (sounds
  like"muscle")

  *The shell of this
  steamed mussel
  didn't open.*

must

mus•tache (*or*
  mous•tache)

mus•tang

mus•tard

must•n't

must•y

mu•tant

mu•tate

mu•**ta**•tion

mute

mu•ti•late

mu•ti•**la**•tion

mu•ti•nies

mu•ti•nous

mu•ti•ny

mutt

mut•ter

mut•ton

mu•tu•al

muz•zle

muz•zling

my

my•nah (*or* **my**•na)

my•ri•ad

my•**self**

mys•ter•ies

mys•**te**•ri•ous

mys•ter•y

mys•ti•fy

myth

myth•i•cal

myth•o•**log**•i•cal

my•**thol**•o•gies

my•**thol**•o•gy

N

nab

nabbed

nab·bing

nag

Na·ga·**sa**·ki

nagged

nag·ging

nail

na·**ive**

na·ked

na·ked·ness

name

nam·ing

nan·nies

nan·ny

nap

nap·kin

nar·**cis**·sus

nar·**cot**·ic

nar·rate

nar·ra·tive

nar·row

na·sal

nas·ti·er

nas·ti·est

nas·ti·ness

nas·**tur**·tium

nas·ty

na·tion

na·tion·al

na·tion·al·ism

na·tion·al·ist

na·tion·al·**is**·tic

na·tion·**al**·i·ties

na·tion·**al**·i·ty

na·tion·al·ize

na·tion·al·iz·ing

na·tive

Na·tive A·**mer**·i·can

Na·**tiv**·i·ty

nat·u·ral

nat·u·ral·ist

nat·u·ral·ize

nat·u·ral·ly

na·ture

naugh·ti·er

naught·i·est

naugh·ti·ness

naught·y

nau·se·a

narcissus

nau·se·ate

nau·se·at·ing

nau·seous

nau·ti·cal

Na·va·jo (or **Na**·va·ho)

na·val (sounds like "navel")

England was a great naval power.

na·vel (sounds like "naval")

Your navel is your belly button.

nav·i·ga·ble

nav·i·gate

nav·i·gat·ing

nav·i·**ga**·tion

nav·i·ga·tor

na·vy

Na·zi

Na·zi·sm

Ne·**an**·der·thal

near

near·by

near·ly

near·**sight**·ed

neat

neat·ness

Ne·**bras**·ka

neb·u·la (sing.)

neb·u·lae (pl.)

neb·u·las (pl.)

neb·u·lous
nec·es·**sar**·i·ly
nec·es·sar·y
ne·**ces**·si·tate
ne·**ces**·si·ties
ne·**ces**·si·ty
neck
neck·er·chief
neck·lace
neck·tie
nec·tar
need (sounds like
  "knead")
  I need a nickel.
need·ed
need·i·er
need·i·est
nee·dle
need·less
need·less·ly
nee·dle·work
need·n't
need·y
neg·a·tive
neg·**lect**
neg·**lect**·ful
neg·li·gence
neg·li·gent
ne·**go**·tia·ble
ne·**go**·ti·ate
ne·**go**·ti·at·ing
ne·go·ti·**a**·tion
ne·**go**·ti·a·tor
neigh

neigh·bor
neigh·bor·hood
neigh·bor·ly
nei·ther

(**newborn**)

ne·on
neph·ew
Nep·tune
nerd
nerve
nerv·ous
nest
nes·tle
nes·tling
net
net·ted
net·ting
net·work
neu·ter

neu·tral
neu·**tral**·i·ty
neu·tra·lize
neu·tron
Ne·**vad**·a
nev·er
nev·er·**more**
nev·er·the·**less**
new
new·born
new·com·er
New **Eng**·land
New·found·land
New Hamp·shire
New Jer·sey
New Mex·i·co
news
news·cast
news·cast·er
news·let·ter
news·pa·per
news·print
news·stand
newt
New Tes·ta·ment
New York
New Zea·land
next
Ni·**ag**·a·ra
nib·ble
nib·bling
Nic·a·**ra**·gua
nice
nic·er

nic•est

niche

nick

nick•el

nick•name

nic•o•tine

niece

night (sounds like "knight")

Last night it was very warm.

night•fall

night•gown

night•in•gale

night•ly

night•mare

nim•ble

nine

nine•ty

nin•ja

ninth

nip

nipped

nip•ple

nit (sounds like "knit")

Please pick the nit out of my hair.

ni•tro•gen

no (sounds like "know")

No, thank you.

no•bil•i•ty

no•ble

no•ble•man

no•ble•ness

no•blesse o•blige

no•ble•wom•an

no•bly

no•bod•ies

no•bod•y

noc•tur•nal

nod

nod•ded

nod•ding

noise

nois•y

no•mad

no•mad•ic

nom•i•nate

nom•i•nat•ing

nom•i•na•tion

nom•i•nee

non•com•mit•tal

none•the•less

non•fic•tion

non•sense

non•stop

noo•dle

noon

no one

noose

nor

nor•mal

nor•mal•cy

nor•mal•i•ty

north

North A•mer•i•ca

North Car•o•li•na

North Da•ko•ta

North•east

North•ern Hem•i•sphere

North•west

Nor•way

Nor•we•gian

nose

nos•tal•gia

nos•tal•gic

nos•tril

nos•y

not (sounds like "knot")

I will not do that!

no•ta•ble

no•ta•bly

no•ta•tion

notch

note

note•book

noth•ing

no•tice

no•tice•able

no•tice•a•bly

no•ticed

no•tic•ing

no•ti•fi•ca•tion

no•ti•fied

no•ti•fies

no•ti•fy

no•tion

no•to•ri•e•ty

no•to•ri•ous

noun
nour•ish
nour•ish•ment
nov•el
nov•el•ties
nov•el•ty
No•**vem**•ber
nov•ice
no•vo•caine
now
no•where
noz•zle
nu•cle•ar
nu•cle•us
nude
nudge

nudg•ing
nud•ist
nug•get
nui•sance
numb
num•ber
nu•mer•al
nu•mer•a•tor
nu•**mer**•i•cal
nu•mer•ous
nun
nup•tial
nurse
nurs•er•ies
nurs•er•y
nurs•ing

nur•ture
nur•tur•ing
nut
nut•crack•er
nut•meg
nu•tri•ent
nu•**tri**•tion
nu•**tri**•tious
nut•shell
nut•tier
nut•tiest
nut•ti•ness
nuz•zle
nuz•zling
ny•lon
nymph

O

oak
oar
oar•lock
o•**a**•ses (pl.)
o•**a**•sis (sing.)
oat
oath
oat•meal
o•**be**•di•ence
o•**be**•di•ent
ob•**ese**
o•**bes**•i•ty
o•**bey**
o•**bit**•u•ar•ies
o•**bit**•u•ar•y
ob•**ject** (v.)
ob•ject (n.)
ob•**jec**•tion
ob•**jec**•tive
ob•li•gate
ob•li•**ga**•tion
o•**blige**
o•**blig**•ing
ob•**liv**•i•on
ob•**liv**•i•ous
ob•long
ob•**nox**•ious
o•boe
o•bo•ist
ob•**scene**
ob•**scen**•i•ties
ob•**scen**•i•ty

ob•**scure**
ob•**serv**•ance
ob•**serv**•ant
ob•ser•**va**•tion
ob•**serv**•a•to•ries
ob•**serv**•a•to•ry
ob•**serve**
ob•**serv**•ing
ob•**sess**
ob•**ses**•sion
ob•**ses**•sive
ob•so•lete
  also pronounced
  ob•so•**lete**
ob•sta•cle
ob•ste•**tri**•cian
ob•sti•nate
ob•**struct**

o•cean•**og**•ra•pher
o•cean•**og**•ra•phy
oce•lot
o'**clock**
oc•ta•gon
oc•**tag**•o•nal
oc•ta•**he**•dron
oc•tave
Oc•**to**•ber
oc•to•ge•**nar**•i•an
oc•to•pus
odd
odd•i•ty
odds

ob•**struc**•tion
ob•**tain**
ob•**tuse**
ob•vi•ous
oc•**ca**•sion
oc•**ca**•sio•nal
oc•cu•pan•cy
oc•cu•pant
oc•cu•**pa**•tion
oc•cu•**pa**•tion•al
oc•cu•pi•er
oc•cu•py
oc•**cur**
oc•**curred**
oc•**cur**•rence
oc•**cur**•ring
o•cean
o•ce•**an**•ic

oboist

135

ode (sounds like "owed")

My poem is an ode to nature.

o•di•ous

o•dor

Od•ys•sey

of

off

of•**fend**

of•**fend**•er

of•**fense**

of•**fen**•sive

of•fer

of•fer•ing

off•hand

of•fice

of•fi•cer

of•**fi**•cial

off-peak

off•side

off•spring

off-the-wall

of•ten

o•gre

oh

O•hi•o

ohm

oil

oint•ment

O•**jib**•wa

o•**kay** (*or* **OK**)

o•**kayed**

Ok•la•**ho**•ma

ok•ra

old

old•en

old-fash•ioned

Old Tes•ta•ment

O•**lym**•pics

om•**buds**•man

also pronounced
om•buds•man

om•e•let (*or*
om•e•lette)

o•men

om•i•nous

o•**mis**•sion

o•**mit**

o•**mit**•tance

o•**mit**•ted

(**opera**)

o•**mit**•ting

om•ni•bus

om•ni•vore

once

on•com•ing

one (sounds like "won")

One minute, please!

one-sid•ed

one-way

on•go•ing

on•ion

on-line

on•ly

on•o•mat•o•**poe**•ia

on•set

on•to

on•ward

on•wards

ooze

ooz•ing

o•pal

o•**paque**

o•pen

o•pen•ing

op•er•a

op•er•ate

op•er•**at**•ic

op•er•at•ing

op•er•**a**•tion

op•er•**a**•tion•al

op•er•a•tor

op•er•**et**•ta

oph•thal•**mol**•o•gist

oph•thal•**mol**•o•gy
o•**pin**•ion
o•**pin**•ion•at•ed
o•**pos**•sum
op•**po**•nent
op•por•**tu**•ni•ties
op•por•**tu**•ni•ty
op•**pose**
op•**pos**•ing
op•po•site
op•po•**si**•tion
op•**press**
opt
op•ti•cal
op•**ti**•cian
op•ti•mism
op•ti•mist
op•ti•**mis**•tic
op•ti•mum
op•tion
op•tion•al
op•**tom**•e•trist
or
o•ral (sounds like
   "aural")
   An oral report is
   spoken.
or•ange
o•**rang**•u•tan
or•bit
or•chard
or•ches•tra
or•ches•**tra**•tion
or•chid

or•**dain**
or•**deal**
or•der
or•der•ly
or•di•nal
or•di•**nar**•i•ly
or•di•**nar**•y
ore
Or•e•gon
or•gan
or•**gan**•ic
or•**gan**•i•cal•ly
or•gan•ism
or•gan•ist
or•gan•i•**za**•tion
or•gan•ize
or•gan•iz•ing
o•**ri**•ent
o•ri•en•**ta**•tion
o•ri•**ga**•mi
or•i•gin
o•**rig**•i•nal
o•**rig**•i•nate
o•ri•ole
or•na•ment
or•na•**men**•tal
or•**nate**
or•ni•**thol**•o•gist
or•ni•**thol**•o•gy
or•phan
or•phan•age
or•tho•**don**•tist
or•tho•dox
or•tho•dox•y

os•**mo**•sis
os•trich
oth•er
oth•er•wise
ot•ter
ouch
ought
ounce
our
ours
our•**selves**
oust
out
out•break
out•burst
out•cast
out•come
out•cry
out•**dat**•ed
out•**do**
out•**doors**
out•er
out•fit
out•fit•ted
out•fit•ting
out•go•ing
out•**grow**
out•ing
out•law
out•let
out•line
out•look
out•**num**•ber
out-of-date

out•pa•tient
out•post
out•put
out•rage
out•ra•geous
out•right
out•set
out•side (adv. and prep.)
out•side (n.)
out•skirts
out•smart
out•spo•ken
out•stand•ing
out•ward
out•wit
out•wit•ted
out•wit•ting
o•val
o•va•ries
o•va•ry
o•va•tion
ov•en
o•ver
o•ver•all
o•ver•alls
o•ver•bear•ing
o•ver•board
o•ver•came
o•ver•cast
o•ver•coat
o•ver•come

o•ver•com•ing
o•ver•dose
o•ver•draft
o•ver•drawn
o•ver•due
o•ver•eat
o•ver•flow
o•ver•grown
o•ver•hand
o•ver•haul
o•ver•head (adv.)
o•ver•head (adj. and n.)
o•ver•hear
o•ver•joyed
o•ver•lap
o•ver•lapped
o•ver•lap•ping
o•ver•load (v.)
o•ver•load (n.)
o•ver•look
o•ver•ly
o•ver•night (adv.)
o•ver•night (adj.)
o•ver•pass
o•ver•pop•u•la•ted
o•ver•pop•u•la•tion
o•ver•pow•er
o•ver•rat•ed
o•ver•re•ac•tion
o•ver•rule
o•ver•run

o•ver•run•ning
o•ver•seas
o•ver•sleep
o•ver•slept
o•ver•take
o•ver•throw
o•ver•time
o•ver•ture
o•ver•turn
o•ver•weight
o•ver•whelm
o•ver•work
owe
owed (sounds like "ode")
I owed my brother two dollars.
ow•ing
owl
own
own•er
own•er•ship
ox
ox•i•da•tion
ox•i•dize
ox•i•diz•ing
ox•y•gen
ox•y•mo•ron
oy•ster
o•zone

P

pace
pace•mak•er
pach•y•derm
pa•**cif**•ic
Pa•**cif**•ic **O**•cean
pac•i•fied
pac•i•fi•er
pac•i•fies
pac•i•fism
pac•i•fist
pac•i•fy
pack
pack•age
pack•ag•ing
pack•et
pact
pad
pad•ded
pad•dies
pad•ding
pad•dle
pad•dy
pad•lock
pa•gan
page
pag•eant
pag•eant•ry
pag•er
pag•ing
pa•**go**•da
pail (sounds like "pale")

I knocked over the pail of water.

pain
pain•ful
pain•kill•er
pain•less
pains•tak•ing
paint
paint•brush
paint•er
pair (sounds like "pare" and "pear")

I lost a pair of socks.

pa•**ja**•mas
pal
pal•ace
pal•ate (sounds like "palette")

paddle

Peanut butter sticks to my palate.

pale (sounds like "pail")

She looks pale and sick.

pale•ness
pa•le•on•**tol**•o•gist
pa•le•on•**tol**•o•gy
Pa•le•o•**zo**•ic
Pal•es•tine
pal•ette (sounds like "palate")

The painter put bright colors on his palette.

pal•in•drome
pal•i•**sade**
palm
pal•**met**•to
palm•ist•ry
pal•o•**mi**•no
pam•pas
pam•per
pam•phlet
pan
pan•cake
pan•cre•as
pan•da
pan•de•**mo**•ni•um
pane
pan•el
pan•el•ist

pang
pan·ic
pan·icked
pan·ick·ing
pan·ick·y
pan·ic-**strick**·en
panned
pan·o·**ram**·a
pan·o·**ram**·ic
pan·sies
pan·sy
pant
pan·ther
pan·ties
pan·to·mime
pan·tries
pan·try
pants
pan·ty
pa·**pa**·ya
pa·per
pa·per·back
pa·per·weight
pa·per·work
pa·pier-mâ·**ché**
pa·**poose**
pap·**ri**·ka
  also pronounced
  pap·ri·ka
pa·**py**·rus
par
par·a·ble
par·a·chute
par·a·chut·ing

pa·**rade**
pa·**rad**·ing
par·a·dise
par·a·dox
par·a·**dox**·i·cal
par·af·fin
par·a·graph
par·a·keet
par·a·**le**·gal
par·al·lel
par·al·**lel**·o·gram
pa·**ral**·y·sis
par·a·lyze
par·a·lyz·ing
par·a·**me**·ci·a (pl.)
par·a·**me**·ci·um
  (sing.)
par·a·mount
par·a·**pher**·na·lia
par·a·phrase
par·a·phras·ing

parachuting

par·a·**ple**·gic
par·a·site
par·a·**sit**·ic
par·a·sol
par·a·troop·er
par·cel
parch
parch·ment
par·don
pare (sounds like "pair"
  and "pear")
  Use a knife to pare
  the apple.
par·ent
pa·**ren**·the·ses (pl.)
pa·**ren**·the·sis (sing.)
par·ing
par·ish
pa·**rish**·ion·er
park
par·ka
park·way
par·lia·ment
par·lia·**men**·ta·ry
par·lor
Par·me·san
pa·**ro**·chi·al
par·o·dies
par·o·dy
pa·**role**
par·rot
pars·ley
pars·nip
par·son

part
Par•the•non
par•tial
par•ti•**al**•i•ty
par•**tic**•i•pant
par•**tic**•i•pate
par•**tic**•i•pat•ing
par•tic•i•**pa**•tion
par•ti•ci•ple
par•ti•cle
par•**tic**•u•lar
par•ties
part•ing
par•**ti**•tion
part•ly
part•ner
par•tridge
part-time
par•ty
pass
pas•sage
pas•sage•way
pas•sen•ger
pas•ser•by
pas•sion
pas•sion•ate
pas•sive
Pass•o•ver
pass•port
pass•word
past
pas•ta
paste
pas•**tel**

pas•teur•i•**za**•tion
pas•teur•ize
pas•ti•er
pas•ti•est
pas•time
pas•ti•ness
pas•tor
pas•tor•al
pas•try
pas•ture
pat
patch
patch•work
patch•y
pâ•**té**
pat•ent
pat•**er**•nal
pat•**er**•ni•ty
path
pa•**thet**•ic
pa•**thet**•i•cal•ly
path•o•**log**•i•cal
pa•**thol**•o•gist
pa•**thol**•o•gy
pa•tience
pa•tient
pat•i•o
pat•i•os
pa•**tri**•arch
pa•**tri**•ot
pa•tri•**ot**•ic
pa•tri•ot•ism
pa•**trol**
pa•**trolled**

pa•**trol**•ling
pa•tron
pa•tron•age
pa•tron•ize
pa•tron•iz•ing
pat•ted
pat•ter
pat•tern
pat•ties
pat•ting
pat•ty
pau•per
pause
paus•ing
pave
pave•ment
pa•**vil**•ion
pav•ing
paw
pawn
pawn•brok•er
pay
pay•roll
pea
peace (sounds like
    "piece")
    The countries
    signed a peace
    treaty.
peace•a•ble
peace•ful
peace•ful•ly
peace•mak•er
peace•time

peach

pea•cock

peak (sounds like
"peek")

*She's at the peak
of her game.*

peal (sounds like
"peel")

*At noon, the bells
peal.*

pea•nut

pea•nut **but**•ter

pear (sounds like "pair"
and "pare")

*You eat the pear, and
I'll eat the apple.*

pearl

peas•ant

peat

peb•ble

pe•can
also pronounced
pe•**can**

peck

pe•**cu**•liar

pe•cu•li•**ar**•i•ties

pe•cu•li•**ar**•i•ty

ped•al (sounds like
"peddle")

Pedal the bike slowly.

ped•dle (sounds like
"pedal")

*Can I peddle this for
two dollars?*

ped•dler

ped•dling

ped•es•tal

pe•**des**•tri•an

pe•di•a•**tric**•ian

ped•i•gree

peek (sounds like
"peak")

*Don't peek behind
the door.*

peel (sounds like
"peal")

Peel the apple, please.

peep

peer (sounds like
"pier")

*Your classmate is
your peer.*

peg

Pe•king•**ese**

pel•i•can

pel•let

pell-mell

pelt

pen

pe•nal•ize

pen•al•ties

pen•al•ty

pen•cil

pen•dant

pen•du•lum

pen•e•trate

pen•e•trat•ing

pen•e•**tra**•tion

pen•guin

pen•i•**cil**•lin

pen•**in**•su•la

pen•i•tence

pen•i•tent

pen•i•**ten**•tia•ries

pen•i•**ten**•tia•ry

pen•knife

pen•knives

pen name

pen•nant

pen•nies

pen•ni•less

pen•ning

Penn•syl•**va**•nia

pen•ny

pen pal

pen•sion

pen•ta•gon

pen•**tag**•o•nal

pent•house

pe•o•ny

peo•ple

pep

pepped

pep•per

pep•per•mint

pep•per•y

pep•ping

per (sounds like
"purr")

*They charge a dime
per apple.*

per•**ceive**

per•**ceiv**•ing

per•**cent**
per•**cent**•age
per•**cep**•ti•ble
per•**cep**•tion
per•**cep**•tive
perch
per•**chance**
per•**cus**•sion
per•**cus**•sion•ist
per•**en**•nial
per•e•**stroi**•ka
per•fect (adj.)
per•**fect** (v.)
per•**fec**•tion
per•**form**
per•**form**•ance
per•**form**•er
per•fume
  also pronounced
  per•**fume**
per•**haps**
per•il
per•i•lous
pe•**rim**•e•ter
pe•ri•od
pe•ri•**od**•ic
pe•ri•**od**•i•cal
pe•**riph**•er•al
pe•**riph**•er•ies
pe•**riph**•er•y
per•i•scope
per•ish
per•ish•a•ble
per•jure

per•**ju**•ry
perk
perk•y
perm
per•ma•nence
per•ma•nent
per•me•ate
per•**mis**•si•ble
per•**mis**•sion
per•**mis**•sive
per•**mis**•sive•ness
per•**mit** (v.)
per•mit (n.)
per•**mit**•ted
per•**mit**•ting
per•mu•**ta**•tion
per•pen•**dic**•u•lar
per•**pet**•u•al
per•**pet**•u•ate

periscope

per•**pet**•u•at•ing
per•**plex**
per•**plex**•i•ties
per•**plex**•i•ty
per•se•cute
per•se•cut•ing
per•se•**cu**•tion
per•se•**ver**•ance
per•se•**vere**
per•se•**ver**•ing
Per•sia
per•**sim**•mon
per•**sist**
per•**sist**•ence
per•**sist**•ent
per•son
per•son•al
per•son•**al**•i•ties
per•son•**al**•i•ty
per•son•al•ly
per•son•**nel**
per•**spec**•tive
per•spi•**ra**•tion
per•**spire**
per•**spir**•ing
per•**suade**
per•**suad**•ing
per•**sua**•sion
per•**sua**•sive
per•**tain**
per•ti•nent
per•**turb**
Pe•**ru**
per•**verse**

per•**ver**•si•ty
pe•**se**•ta
pe•so
pes•si•mism
pes•si•mist
pes•si•**mis**•tic
pest
pes•ter
pes•ti•cide
pes•tle
pet
pet•al
pe•**ti**•tion
pet•ri•fied
pe•**tro**•le•um
pet•ti•coat
pet•ting
pet•ty
pe•**tu**•nia
pew
pew•ter
phan•tom
phar•aoh
phar•ma•cies
phar•ma•cist
phar•ma•cy
phase
pheas•ant
phe•**nom**•e•na
phe•**nom**•e•nal
phe•**nom**•e•non
phe•**nom**•e•nons
phil•**an**•thro•pist
phil•**an**•thro•py

phil•o•**den**•dron
phil•o•**soph**•i•cal
phi•**los**•o•phy
phlegm
pho•bi•a
pho•bic
phone
pho•**net**•i•cal•ly
pho•**net**•ics
pho•no•graph
phos•pho•**res**•cence
phos•pho•**res**•cent
phos•pho•rus
pho•to
pho•to•cop•i•er
pho•to•cop•ies
pho•to•cop•y
pho•to•cop•y•ing
pho•to•**gen**•ic
pho•to•graph
pho•**to**•gra•pher
pho•to•**graph**•ic
pho•**to**•gra•phy
pho•to•**jour**•nal•ism
pho•to•**jour**•nal•ist
pho•to•**syn**•the•sis
phrase
phys•i•cal
phy•**si**•cian
phys•i•cist
phys•ics
pi (sounds like "pie")
  *π stands for pi
  in math.*

pi•**an**•ist
  also pronounced
  pi•a•nist

(**piano**)

pi•**an**•o
pi•**an**•os
pic•co•lo
pic•co•los
pick
pick•ax (*or* **pick**•axe)
pick•er•el
pick•et
pick•et•er
pick•i•er
pick•i•est
pick•le
pick•pock•et
pick•up

pick•y
pic•nic
pic•nicked
pic•nick•ing
pic•to•graph
pic•**to**•ri•al
pic•ture
pic•tur•**esque**
pie (sounds like "pi")

*Cherry pie is my
favorite dessert.*

piece (sounds like
"peace")

*May I have a piece
of pie?*

piece•work
pier (sounds like
"peer")

*Don't stand on the
edge of the pier.*

pierce
pierc•ing
pi•e•ty
pig
pi•geon
pig•gy•back
pig•gy **bank**
pig•ment
pig•pen
pig•sties
pig•sty
pig•tail
pike
pile

pil•grim
pil•grim•age
pill
pil•lar
pil•low
pil•low•case
pi•lot
pim•ple
pin
pi•**ña**•ta
pin•ball
pin•cer
pinch
pin•cush•ion
pine
pine•ap•ple
Ping-Pong
pin•ing
pink
pink•eye
pin•point
pin•stripe
pint
pin•to
pin•tos
pin•wheel
pi•o•**neer**
pi•ous
pipe
pipe•line
pip•ing
pi•rate
pi•rat•ing
pis•**ta**•chio

pis•til (sounds like
"pistol")

*The pistil is the female
part of the flower.*

pis•tol (sounds like
"pistil")

*Did you hear a
pistol shot?*

pis•ton
pit
pi•ta
pitch
pitch•er
pitch•fork
pit•fall
pit•ied
pit•ies
pit•i•ful
pit•i•less
pit•ted
pit•y
pit•y•ing
piv•ot
piv•ot•al
pix•el
pix•ie (*or* pix•y)
pix•ies
piz•za
pla•cate
pla•cat•ing
place
plac•id
plac•ing
pla•gia•rism

pla•gia•rist
pla•gia•rize
pla•gia•riz•ing
plague
pla•guing
plaid
plain (sounds like "plane")

I like things plain, not fancy.

plain•tive
plait
plan
plane (sounds like "plain")

The plane was delayed by fog.

plan•et
plan•e•tar•i•um
plan•e•tar•y
plank
plank•ton
planned
plan•ning
plant
plan•tain
plan•ta•tion
plaque
plas•ma
plas•ter
plas•ter•er
plas•tic
plate
pla•teau

plate•let
plat•form
plat•ing
plat•i•num
Pla•to
pla•toon
plat•ter
plat•y•pus
plau•si•ble
play
play•er
play•ful
play•ful•ly
play•ground
play•mate
play•pen
play•room
play•wright
pla•za
plea
plead
pleas•ant
please
pleased
pleas•ing
pleas•ur•a•ble
pleas•ure
pleat
pleat•ed
pledge
pledg•ing
plen•ti•ful
plen•ty
pli•a•ble

pli•ers
plight
plod
plot
plo•ver
plow
pluck
pluck•i•ly
pluck•i•ness
pluck•y
plug
plugged
plug•ging
plum (sounds like "plumb")

I ate a small, ripe plum.

plum•age
plumb (sounds like "plum")

I felt plumb stupid.

plumb•er
plumb•ing
plume
plump
plun•der
plun•der•er
plunge
plung•ing
plu•ral
plus
Plu•to
plu•to•ni•um
ply•wood

pneu•**mat**•ic
pneu•**mo**•nia
poach
poach•er
pock•et
pock•et•book
pock•et•knife
pod
po•em
po•et
po•**et**•ic
po•et•ry
poin•**set**•ti•a
point
point-blank
point•less
point of view
poise
poised
poi•son
poi•son i•vy
poi•son•ous
poi•son **su**•mac
poke
pok•er
po•lar
pole (sounds like
   "poll")
*She hitched her pony
to the pole.*
pole•cat
pole vault
po•**lice**
po•**lice**•man

po•**lice of**•fi•cer
po•**lice**•wom•an
pol•i•cies
pol•i•cy
po•li•o
pol•ish
pol•ished
po•**lite**
po•**lite**•ness
pol•i•**ti**•cian
pol•i•tics
pol•ka
pol•ka **dot**
poll (sounds like
   "pole")
*The poll showed he
would win the
election.*
pol•len
pol•li•nate
pol•li•nat•ing
pol•li•**na**•tion
pol•**lut**•ant
pol•**lute**
pol•**lut**•er
pol•**lut**•ing
pol•**lu**•tion
po•lo
pol•y•**es**•ter
pol•y•gon
pol•y•mer
pol•yp
pol•y•**sty**•rene
pol•y•un•**sat**•u•rates

pomp
pomp•ous
pon•cho
pond
pon•der
pon•der•ous
po•ny
Po•ny Ex•**press**
po•ny•tail
poo•dle

(**poodle**)

pool
poor (sounds like
   "pore" and "pour")
*Once I was poor;
now I'm rich.*
poor•ly
pop
pop•corn
pope
pop•lar

P

pop•py
pop•u•lar
pop•u•**lar**•i•ty
pop•u•lar•ly
pop•u•late
pop•u•lat•ing
pop•u•**la**•tion
por•ce•lain
porch
por•cu•pine
pore (sounds like
  "poor" and "pour")
*A pore is a tiny hole
in your skin.*
pork
po•rous
por•poise
por•ridge
port
port•a•ble
por•ter
port•**fol**•i•o
port•hole
por•tion
port•ly
por•trait
por•**tray**
por•**tray**•al
pose
posh
pos•ing
po•**si**•tion
pos•i•tive
pos•se

pos•**sess**
pos•**ses**•sion
pos•**ses**•sive
pos•si•**bil**•i•ty
pos•si•ble
pos•sum

(**possum**)

post
post•age
post•al
post•card
post•er
post•hu•mous
post•man
post•mark
post•mast•er
post•mis•tress
post of•fice

post•**pone**
post•**pone**•ment
post•**pon**•ing
post•script
pos•ture
post•**war**
pot
po•**tas**•si•um
po•**ta**•to
po•**ta**•toes
po•ten•cy
po•tent
po•**ten**•tial
pot•hole
pot•ter
pot•ter•y
pouch
poul•try
pounce
pounc•ing
pound
pour (sounds like
  "poor" and "pore")
*Please pour me
some milk.*
pout
pov•er•ty
pow•der
pow•der•y
pow•er
pow•er•ful
pow•er•less
prac•ti•cal
prac•ti•**cal**•i•ty

prac·ti·cal·ly
prac·tice
prac·tic·ing
prai·rie
prai·rie **schoo**·ner
praise
prais·ing
prance
pranc·ing
prank
pray (sounds like
  "prey")
  *Let's pray it won't
  rain on our picnic.*
pray·er
pray·ing **man**·tis
preach
pre·**car**·i·ous
pre·**cau**·tion
pre·**cede**
pre·ce·dence
pre·ce·dent
pre·**ced**·ing
pre·cinct
pre·cious
prec·i·pice
pre·**cip**·i·tate
pre·**cip**·i·tating
pre·cip·i·**ta**·tion
pre·**cise**
pre·**cise**·ly
pre·**co**·cious
pred·a·tor
pred·e·ces·sor

pre·**dic**·a·ment
pred·i·cate
pre·**dict**
pre·**dic**·tion
pre·**dom**·i·nate
pre·**dom**·i·nat·ing
preen
pre·face
pre·**fer**
pref·er·ence
pre·**ferred**
pre·**fer**·ring
pre·fix
preg·nan·cy
preg·nant
pre·his·**tor**·ic
pre·**his**·tor·y
prej·u·dice
pre·**lim**·i·nar·y
pre·ma·**ture**
pre·**med**·i·tat·ed
pre·**mier** (sounds like
  "premiere")
  *The French
  government has a
  new premier.*
pre·**miere** (sounds like
  "premier")
  *Many famous movie
  stars attended the
  premiere.*
prem·ise
prem·is·es
pre·mi·um

pre·mo·**ni**·tion
pre·**oc**·cu·pied
prep·a·**ra**·tion
pre·**pare**
pre·**par**·ing
prep·o·**si**·tion
pre·**pos**·ter·ous
prep school
pre·school
pre·**scribe**
pre·**scrib**·ing
pre·**scrip**·tion
pres·ence
pre·sent (n.)
pre·**sent** (v.)
pres·en·**ta**·tion
pres·ent·ly
pre·**serv**·a·tive
pre·**serve**
pre·**serv**·ing
pre·**side**
pres·i·den·cy
pres·i·dent
pres·i·dent-e·**lect**
pres·i·**den**·tial
pre·**sid**·ing
press
pres·sing
pres·sure
pres·sur·ing
pres·sur·ize
pres·sur·iz·ing
pres·**tige**
pres·**ti**·gious

pre•**sum**•a•bly
pre•**sume**
pre•**sum**•ing
pre•**sump**•tion
pre•**tend**
pre•tense
  also pronounced
  pre•**tense**
pre•text
pret•ti•er
pret•ti•est
pret•ti•ly
pret•ti•ness
pret•ty
pret•zel
pre•**vail**
prev•a•lent
pre•**vent**
pre•**ven**•tion
pre•**ven**•tive
pre•view
pre•vi•ous
prey (sounds like
  "pray")
  *Owls often prey
  on mice.*
price
price•less
pric•ing
prick
prick•le
prick•ly
pride
pried

pries
priest
priest•hood
priest•ly
prim
pri•ma **don**•na
pri•**mar**•i•ly
pri•mar•y
pri•mate
prime
pri•**me**•val
prim•i•tive
prim•rose
prince
prince•ly
prin•cess
prin•ci•pal (sounds like
  "principle")
  *The principal is in
  the office.*
prin•ci•ple (sounds like
  "principal")
  *Please explain the
  principle of gravity.*
print
print•out
pri•or
pri•**or**•i•ties
pri•**or**•i•ty
prism
pris•on
pris•on•er
pri•va•cy
pri•vate

priv•i•lege
prize
pro
prob•a•**bil**•i•ty
prob•a•ble
pro•bate
pro•bat•ing
pro•**ba**•tion
probe
prob•ing
prob•lem
pro•**ce**•dure
pro•**ceed**
pro•ceeds
proc•ess
pro•**ces**•sion
proc•es•sor
pro•**claim**
proc•la•**ma**•tion
pro•**cras**•ti•nate
pro•**cras**•ti•nat•ing
pro•cras•ti•**na**•tion
pro•**cras**•ti•na•tor
prod
prod•ded
prod•ding
prod•i•gal
prod•i•gies
prod•i•gy
pro•**duce** (v.)
pro•duce (n.)
pro•**duc**•er
pro•**duc**•ing
prod•uct

pro•**duc**•tion
pro•**duc**•tive
pro•duc•**tiv**•i•ty
pro•**fess**
pro•**fes**•sion
pro•**fes**•sion•al
pro•**fes**•sor
pro•**fi**•cien•cy
pro•**fi**•cient
pro•file
pro•fit (sounds like "prophet")

We made a profit on our car wash.

prof•it•a•ble
pro•**found**
pro•gram
pro•grammed
pro•gram•mer
pro•gram•ming
prog•ress
pro•**gres**•sion
pro•**gress**•ive
pro•**hib**•it
pro•hi•**bi**•tion
proj•ect (n.)
pro•**ject** (v.)
pro•**jec**•tile
pro•**jec**•tion
pro•**jec**•tor
pro•**li**•fic
pro•logue
pro•**long**
prom•e•**nade**

propeller

prom•e•**nad**•ing
prom•ise
prom•ised
prom•ises
prom•is•ing
pro•**mote**
pro•**mot**•ing
pro•**mo**•tion
prompt
prompt•er
prone
prong
pro•noun
pro•**nounce**
pro•**nounce**•ment
pro•**nounc**•ing
pro•nun•ci•**a**•tion
proof
proof•read
prop

prop•a•**gan**•da
pro•**pel**
pro•**pel**•lant
pro•**pelled**
pro•**pel**•ler
pro•**pel**•ling
prop•er
prop•er•ly
prop•er•ties
prop•er•ty
proph•e•cies
proph•e•cy
proph•et (sounds like "profit")

The prophet predicted war, then peace.

pro•**por**•tion
pro•**por**•tion•al
pro•**pos**•al
pro•**pose**
pro•**pos**•ing
pro•po•**si**•tion
pro•**pul**•sion
prose
pros•e•cute
pros•e•**cu**•tion
pros•e•cu•tor
pros•pect
pro•**spec**•tive
pros•pec•tor
pro•**spec**•tus
pros•per
pros•**per**•i•ty
pros•per•ous

pro•**tect**
pro•**tec**•tion
pro•**tec**•tive
pro•**tec**•tor
pro•tein
pro•test (n.)
pro•**test** (v.)
Prot•es•tant
pro•ton
pro•to•plasm
pro•to•type
pro•to•**zo**•a
pro•to•**zo**•an
pro•**trac**•tor
proud
prove
prov•erb
pro•**vide**
pro•**vid**•er
pro•**vid**•ing
prov•ince
pro•**vin**•cial
prov•ing
pro•**vi**•sion
pro•**voke**
pro•**vok**•ing
prowl
prox•**im**•i•ty
pru•dence
pru•dent
prune
prun•ing
pry
psalm

pseu•do•nym
psy•**chi**•a•trist
psy•**chi**•a•try
psy•chic
psy•cho•**log**•i•cal
psy•**chol**•o•gist
psy•**chol**•o•gy
psy•cho•path
pter•o•**dac**•tyl
pub
pu•ber•ty
pub•lic
pub•li•**ca**•tion
pub•li•cist
pub•**lic**•i•ty
pub•li•cize
pub•li•ciz•ing
pub•lic•ly
pub•lish
pub•lish•er
puck
puck•er
pud•ding
pud•dle
pueb•lo
puff
puf•fin
puf•fy
pug
pug•**na**•cious
pull
pul•ley
pull•o•ver
pulp

pul•pit
pul•sate
pul•sat•ing
pul•**sa**•tion
pu•ma
pum•mel
pump
pump•er•nic•kel
pump•kin

pumpkin

pun
punch
punc•tu•al
punc•tu•**al**•i•ty
punc•tu•**a**•tion
punc•ture
punc•tur•ing
pun•gent
pun•ish

pun•ish•ment
punk
punt
pu•ny
pu•pa (sing.)
pu•pae (pl.)
pu•pil
pup•pet
pup•py
pur•chase
pur•chas•er
pur•chas•ing
pure
pure•bred
pu•**ree**
purge
purg•ing

pu•ri•fi•**ca**•tion
pu•ri•fied
pu•ri•fies
pu•ri•fy
Pur•i•tan
pu•ri•ty
pur•ple
pur•pose
purr (sounds like "per")
Do you hear the
happy cat purr?
purse
purs•ing
pur•**sue**
pur•**su**•er
pur•**su**•ing
pur•**suit**

pus
push
push•er
push•ov•er
push-up
pus•sy
put
pu•trid
putt
put•ter
put•ting
put•ty
puz•zle
puz•zling
py•lon
pyr•a•mid

quack

quad

quad•ran•gle

quad•rant

quad•ri•**lat**•er•al

quad•ru•ped

qua•**dru**•ple

qua•**dru**•plet

quag•mire

quail

quaint

quaint•ness

quake

Quak•er

quak•ing

qual•i•fi•**ca**•tion

qual•i•fied

qual•i•fies

qual•i•fy

qual•i•ties

qual•i•ty

qualm

quan•dar•ies

quan•dar•y

quan•ti•ties

quan•ti•ty

quar•an•tine

quark

quar•rel

quar•rel•some

quar•ries

quar•ry

quart

quar•ter

quar•ter•back

quart•er•ly

quar•**tet**

quartz

qua•sar

qua•ver

quay (sounds like "key")

The boats are unloaded at the quay.

quea•si•er

quea•si•est

quea•si•ness

quea•sy

Que•**bec**

queen

queer

quench

que•ries

que•ry

quest

ques•tion

ques•tion•**naire**

quet•**zal**

queue (sounds like "cue")

We stood in a queue to get on the bus.

quib•ble

quib•bling

quiche

quick

quick•en

quick•ly

quick•sand

quick•sil•ver

quick-tem•pered

quick-wit•ted

qui•et

qui•et•ly

qui•et•ness

quill

quilt

quilt•ed

qui•nine

quin•**tet**

quin•**tup**•let

quip

queen

quipped

quirk

quirk•i•ness

quir•ky

quit

quite

quit•ting

quiv•er

quiz

quizzed

quiz•zes

quiz•zi•cal

quiz•zing

quo•rum

quo•ta

quot•a•ble

quo•ta•tion

quote

quo•tient

quot•ing

Qur'•an (*or* Ko•ran)

rab·bi
rab·bit
ra·bies
rac·**coon**
race
race·track
ra·cial
rac·ing
rac·ist
rack
rack·et (*or* **rac**·quet)
rac·quet·ball
ra·dar
ra·di·al
ra·di·ance
ra·di·ant
ra·di·ate
ra·di·at·ing
ra·di·**a**·tion
ra·di·**a**·tor
rad·i·cal
ra·di·i
ra·di·o
ra·di·o·**ac**·tive
ra·di·o·ac·**tiv**·i·ty
rad·ish
ra·di·um
ra·di·us
ra·don
raf·fle
raft
rag

rage
rag·ged
rag·ged·y
rag·ing
rag·weed
raid
rail
rail·ing
rail·road
rail·way
rain (sounds like
    "reign" and "rein")
    Rain is falling.
rain·bow
rain·coat
rain·drop
rain·fall
rain·y
raise
rai·sin
rais·ing
rake
rak·ing
ral·lies
ral·ly
ral·ly·ing
ram
RAM
Ram·a·dan
ram·ble
ram·bling
ramp

ram·page
ram·pant
ram·part
ram·shack·le
ran
ranch
ran·cid
ran·dom
rang
range
rang·er
rank
ran·sack
ran·som
rant
rap (sounds like
    "wrap")
    We love rap songs.
rap·id
rap·ids
rapped
rap·per
rap·ping
rapt
rare
ras·cal
rash
rasp
rasp·ber·ry
rat
rate
rath·er

rat•i•fi•**ca**•tion
rat•i•fied
rat•i•fies
rat•i•fy
ra•ti•o
ra•tion
ra•tion•al
ra•ti•os
rat•tle
rat•tler
rat•tle•snake
rau•cous
rave
ra•vel
ra•ven
rav•en•ous
ra•**vine**
rav•ing
raw
ray
ray•on
ra•zor
reach
re•**act**
re•**act**•ion
re•**ac**•tor
read
read•a•ble
read•i•ly
read•y
real
re•al•**is**•tic
re•**al**•i•ties
re•**al**•i•ty

re•al•i•**za**•tion
re•al•ize
re•al•iz•ing
re•al•ly
  also pronounced
  real•ly
reap
re•ap•**pear**
re•ap•**pear**•ance
rear
re•ar•**range**
re•ar•**rang**•ing
rea•son
rea•son•a•ble
rea•son•a•bly
rea•son•ing
re•as•**sign**
re•as•**sign**•ing
re•as•**sur**•ance
re•as•**sure**
re•as•**sur**•ing

(**read**)

re•**bel** (v.)
re•bel (n.)
re•**bel**•lion
re•**bel**•lious
re•**boot**
re•**but**
re•**but**•tal
re•**but**•ted
re•**call** (v.)
re•**call** (n.)
  also pronounced
  re•call
re•cap
re•**cede**
re•**ced**•ing
re•**ceipt**
re•**ceive**
re•**ceiv**•er
re•**ceiv**•ing
re•cent
re•**cep**•ta•cle
re•**cep**•tion
re•**cep**•tion•ist
re•cess
  also pronounced
  re•**cess**
re•**ces**•sion
rec•i•pe
re•**cit**•al
re•**cite**
reck•less
reck•on
re•**claim**
re•**cline**

re•**clin**•ing
rec•og•**niz**•a•ble
rec•og•nize
rec•og•niz•ing
re•col•**lect**
rec•ol•**lec**•tion
rec•om•**mend**
rec•om•men•**da**•tion
re•con•**sid**•er
re•con•**struct**
re•con•**struc**•tion
re•**cord** (v.)
rec•ord (n.)
re•**cord**•er
re•**cord**•ing
re•**cov**•er
rec•re•**a**•tion
rec•re•**a**•tion•al
re•**cruit**
re•**cruit**•ment
rec•tan•gle
rec•**tan**•gu•lar
re•**cu**•per•ate
re•**cu**•per•at•ing
re•**cy**•cla•ble
re•**cy**•cle
re•**cy**•cling
red
red•coat
red•den
red•dish
re•**deem**
re•**demp**•tion
re•de•**sign**•ed

red-hand•ed
re•**duce**
re•**duc**•ing
re•**duc**•tion
red•wood
reed
reef
reek (sounds like
   "wreak")
   *Did the house reek
   of onion?*
reel
re•e•**lect**
re•e•**lec**•tion
re•**en**•tries
re•**en**•try
re•**fer**
ref•er•**ee**
ref•er•ence
ref•er•**en**•dum
re•**fer**•ral
re•**ferred**
re•**fer**•ring
re•**fill** (v.)
re•fill (n.)
re•**fine**
re•**fined**
re•**fin**•er•ies
re•**fin**•er•y
re•**fin**•ing
re•**flect**
re•**flec**•tion
re•**flec**•tive
re•**flec**•tor

re•flex
re•**for**•est
re•for•est•**a**•tion
re•**form**
ref•or•**ma**•tion
re•**for**•ma•tor•ies
re•**for**•ma•tor•y
re•**form**•ing
re•**fract**
re•**frac**•tion
re•**frain**
re•**fresh**
re•**fresh**•ments
re•**frig**•er•ate
re•**frig**•er•**a**•tion
re•**frig**•er•a•tor
re•**fu**•el
re•fuge
ref•u•**gee**
   also pronounced
   ref•u•gee
re•**fund** (v.)

reflection

re•fund (n.)
re•**fus**•al
re•**fuse**
ref•use
re•**fus**•ing
re•gal
re•**gard**
re•**gard**•ing
re•**gard**•less
re•**gards**
reg•gae
re•**gime**
reg•i•ment
re•gion
reg•gion•al
reg•is•ter
reg•is•**tra**•tion
re•**gret**
re•**gret**•ful
re•**gret**•ta•ble
re•**gret**•ta•bly
reg•u•lar
reg•u•**lar**•i•ty
reg•u•late
reg•u•lat•ing
reg•u•**la**•tion
re•**gur**•gi•tate
re•**hears**•al
re•**hearse**
re•**hears**•ing
reign (sounds like "rain" and "rein")
The king's reign lasted fifty years.

re•im•**burse**
re•im•**burs**•ing
rein (sounds like "rain" and "reign")
Hold the horse's rein.
rein•deer
re•in•**force**
re•in•**force**•ment
re•in•**forc**•ing
re•**ject** (v.)
re•ject (n.)
re•**jec**•tion
re•**joice**
re•**joic**•ing
re•**late**
re•**lat**•ing
re•**la**•tion
re•**la**•tion•ship
rel•a•tive
rel•a•tive•ly
re•**lax**
re•lax•**a**•tion
re•lay
re•**lease**
re•**leas**•ing
re•**lent**
re•**lent**•less
rel•e•vance
rel•e•vant
re•li•a•**bil**•i•ty
re•**li**•a•ble
re•**li**•a•bly
re•lic
re•**lied**

re•**lief**
re•**lies**
re•**lieve**
re•**lig**•ion
re•**li**•gious
re•lish
re•**luct**•ant
re•**ly**
re•**main**
re•**main**•der
re•**mains**
re•**mark**
re•**mark**•a•ble
re•**mark**•a•bly
re•**me**•di•al
rem•e•dies
rem•e•dy
re•**mem**•ber
re•**mem**•brance
re•**mind**
re•**mind**•er
re•**mod**•el
re•**morse**
re•**morse**•ful
re•**mote**
re•**mote**•ness
re•**move**
re•**mov**•ing
Re•nais•sance
ren•dez•vous
re•**new**
re•**new**•a•ble
ren•o•vate
ren•o•vat•ing

ren•o•**va**•tion
re•**nown**
re•**nowned**
rent
rent•al
re•**paid**
re•**pair**
re•**pay**
re•**pay**•ment
re•**peal**
re•**peat**
re•**pel**
re•**pelled**
re•**pel**•lent
re•**pel**•ling
re•**pent**
re•**pent**•ance
re•**pent**•ant
re•per•**cus**•sion
rep•er•toire
rep•e•**ti**•tion
rep•e•**ti**•tious
re•**pet**•i•tive
re•**place**
re•**place**•ment
re•**plac**•ing
re•**play** (v.)
re•play (n.)
re•**plen**•ish
rep•li•ca
rep•li•cate
re•**plied**
re•**plies**
re•**ply**

re•**ply**•ing
re•**port**
re•**port**•er
rep•re•**sent**
rep•re•sen•**ta**•tion
rep•re•**sent**•a•tive
re•**press**
re•**pres**•sion
re•**prieve**
rep•ri•mand
re•pro•**duce**
re•pro•**duc**•ing
re•pro•**duc**•tion
rep•tile
rep•**til**•i•an
re•**pub**•lic
re•**pub**•li•can
re•**pulse**
re•**pul**•sive
rep•u•ta•ble
rep•u•**ta**•tion
re•**quest**
re•qui•em
re•**quire**
re•**quire**•ment
re•**quir**•ing
re•**read**
re•**run** (v.)
re•run (n.)
res•cue
res•cu•er
re•**search**
  also pronounced
  re•search

re•**sem**•ble
re•**sem**•bling
re•**sent**
re•**sent**•ment
res•er•**va**•tion
re•**serve**
re•**served**
re•**serv**•ing
re•ser•voir
re•**side**
res•i•dence
res•i•dent
res•i•**den**•tial
res•i•due
re•**sign**
res•ig•**na**•tion
re•**signed**
re•**sign**•ing
res•in
re•**sist**
re•**sis**•tance
re•**sis**•tant
res•o•**lu**•tion
re•**solve**
re•**solv**•ing
re•**sort**
re•**source**
  also pronounced
  re•source
re•**source**•ful
re•**spect**
re•**spect**•a•ble
re•**spect**•ful
re•**spec**•tive

res•pi•**ra**•tion
res•pi•ra•to•ry
re•**spond**
re•**sponse**
re•spon•si•**bil**•i•ties
re•spon•si•**bil**•i•ty
re•**spon**•si•ble
re•**spon**•si•bly
rest
res•tau•rant
rest•less
res•to•**ra**•tion
re•**store**
re•**stor**•ing
re•**strain**
re•**straint**
re•**strict**
re•**stric**•tion
re•**stric**•tive
re•**sult**
re•**sume** (often
    confused with
    "resumé")
    *Please resume what
    you were doing.*
re•su•mé (often
    confused with
    "resume")
    *My resumé lists all
    my jobs.*
re•**sus**•ci•tate
re•**sus**•ci•tat•ing
re•**sus**•ci•**ta**•tion
re•**sus**•ci•ta•tor

re•**tail**
re•tail•er
re•**tain**
re•**tard**
re•tar•**da**•tion
ret•i•na
re•**tire**

restaurant

re•**tir**•ing
re•**trace**
re•**treat**
re•**triev**•a•ble
re•**triev**•al
re•**trieve**
re•**triev**•er
re•**triev**•ing
re•**turn**
re•**un**•ion
re•**us**•a•ble
rev

re•**veal**
rev•e•**la**•tion
re•**venge**
rev•e•nue
re•**ver**•ber•ate
rev•er•ence
rev•er•ent
re•**ver**•sal
re•**verse**
re•**vers**•ing
re•**vert**
re•**view**
re•**vise**
re•**vis**•ing
re•**vi**•sion
re•**vive**
re•**viv**•ing
re•**voke**
re•**vok**•ing
re•**volt**
re•**volt**•ing
rev•o•**lu**•tion
rev•o•**lu**•tion•ar•y
re•**volve**
re•**volv**•er
re•**volv**•ing
re•**ward**
re•**ward**•ing
re•**word**
rheu•**mat**•ic **fe**•ver
rheu•ma•tism
rhi•**noc**•er•os
Rhode **Is**•land
rho•do•**den**•dron

rhom•bus

rhu•barb

rhyme

rhym•ing

rhythm

rib

rib•bon

rice

rich

rick•et•y

rick•sha (*or* rick•shaw)

ric•o•chet

rid

rid•dle

ride

ridge

rid•i•cule

ri•**dic**•u•lous

ri•fle

rig

rig•a•ma•role

rigged

rig•ging

right (sounds like
  "write")

  Turn right.

right•eous

right-hand•ed

rig•id

ri•**gid**•i•ty

rim

rind

ring (sounds like
  "wring")

  *I think I heard the
  phone ring.*

ring•lead•er

ring•let

rink

rinse

Ri•o **Gran**•de

ri•ot

rip

ripe

robot

ripped

rip•ping

rip•ple

rise

risk

rit•u•al

ri•val

ri•val•ry

riv•er

road (sounds like
  "rode" and "rowed")

  *The truck drove down
  the road.*

road•run•ner

road•side

roam

roar

roast

rob

rob•ber•y

robe

rob•in

ro•bot

ro•**bot**•ic

ro•**bot**•ics

ro•**bust**

rock

rock•et

rock•ing

rock 'n' **roll**

rod

rode (sounds like
  "road" and "rowed")

  She rode her horse.

ro•dent

ro•de•o

  also pronounced
  ro•**de**•o

roe (sounds like "row")

  Roe are fish eggs.

rogue

role (sounds like "roll")

  *She landed a good role
  in the movie.*

roll (sounds like "role")
Did you eat my roll?
rol•ler
rol•ler **coast**•er
rol•ler-skate (v.)
rol•ler skate (n.)
rol•ler-skat•ing
rol•ling
Ro•man **Cath**•o•lic
ro•**mance**
  also pronounced
  ro•mance
Ro•man **nu**•mer•al
ro•**man**•tic
romp
roof
rook
rook•ie
room
room•mate
room•y
roost
roost•er
root
rope
rose
rose•bud
Rosh Ha•**sha**•na
ros•y
rot
ro•ta•ry
ro•tate
ro•tat•ing
ro•**ta**•tion

rote (sounds like
  "wrote")
  *She learned her times
  tables by rote.*
ro•tor
rot•ten
rouge
rough
rough•age
round
round•a•bout
round•house
round•up
route
rou•tine
row (sounds like "roe")
  Row your boat.
row•boat
row•dy
rowed (sounds like
  "road" and "rode")
  I rowed my boat.
roy•al
roy•al•ty
rub
rub•ber
rub•bish
rub•ble
ru•by
rud•der
rude
ruf•fi•an
ruf•fle
rug

rug•by
rug•ged
ru•in
rule
rul•er
rum
rum•ble
rum•mage
rum•mag•ing
ru•mor
rump
rum•ple
run
run•a•way
run-**down**
rung
run•ner
run•ner-**up**
run•ning
run•ny
run•way
ru•ral
rush
rust
rus•tic
rus•tle
rus•tling
rut
ruth•less
rye (sounds like "wry")
  *I made a sandwich
  with rye bread.*

Sab·bath

sa·ber

sa·ber-**toothed ti**·ger

sa·ble

sab·o·tage

sab·o·tag·ing

sab·o·**teur**

sac (sounds like "sack")

A pouch in an animal's body is a sac.

sac·cha·rin (sounds like "saccharine")

She put saccharin in her tea.

sac·cha·rine (sounds like "saccharin")

Her performance as Melanie was saccharine.

sack (sounds like "sac")

Everything I own is in that sack.

sa·cred

sac·ri·fice

sac·ri·**fi**·cial

sac·ri·fic·ing

sac·ri·lege

sac·ri·le·gious

sad

sad·den

sad·der

sad·dest

sad·dle

sad·dling

sad·ly

sad·ness

sa·**fa**·ri

safe

safe·guard

safe·ty

safe·ty belt

safe·ty pin

sag

sage

sage·brush

sagged

sag·ging

said

sail (sounds like "sale")

The wind filled the boat's sail.

sail·or

saint

Saint Ber·**nard**

saint·ed

sake

sal·ad

sal·a·man·der

sal·a·ries

sal·a·ry

sale (sounds like "sail")

They're having a sale on computers.

sales·man

sales·per·son

sales·wom·an

sa·line

sa·lin·i·ty

sa·li·va

salm·on

sal·mo·**nel**·la

sa·**loon**

sal·sa

salt

salt·wa·ter

sa·**lute**

sa·**lut**·ing

sal·vage

sal·vag·er

sal·vag·ing

sal·**va**·tion

salve

same

sam·ple

sam·pling

sam·u·rai

sanc·tu·aries

sanc·tu·ar·y

sand

san·dal

sand·bag

sand·bar

sand·box

sand·pa·per

sand·pip·er

sand·stone

sand·wich

sand•wich•es
sand•y
sane
san•i•tar•y
san•i•**ta**•tion
san•i•ty
sank
San•ta **Claus**
sap
sap•ling
sapped
sap•phire
sap•ping
sar•casm
sar•**cas**•tic
sar•**dine**
sa•ri
sa•**rong**
sash
Sas•**katch**•e•wan
sat
Sa•tan
satch•el
sat•el•lite
sat•in
sat•ire
sa•**tir**•i•cal
sat•i•rist
sat•is•**fac**•tion
sat•is•**fac**•to•ry
sat•is•fied
sat•is•fies
sat•is•fy
sat•is•fy•ing

sat•u•rate
sat•u•rat•ing
sat•u•**ra**•tion
Sat•ur•day
Sat•urn
sauce
sauce•pan
sau•cer
sau•na
saun•ter
sau•sage
sav•age
sa•**van**•na (or
sa•**van**•nah)
save
sav•ing
sav•ings
sa•vor•y

saw

saw
saw•dust
saw•mill

sax•o•phone
sax•o•phon•ist
say
say•ing
sa•yo•**na**•ra
scab
scab•bard
scaf•fold
scald
scale
scal•ing
scal•lop
scalp
scal•pel
scam•per
scan
scan•dal
scan•dal•ous
Scan•di•**na**•vi•a
Scan•di•**na**•vi•an
scanned
scan•ner
scan•ning
scape•goat
scar
scarce
scarce•ly
scar•ci•ty
scare
scare•crow
scarf
scar•ing
scar•let
scarves

scat·ter
scat·ter·brained
scav·enge
sce·**nar**·i·o
sce·**nar**·i·os
scene (sounds like "seen")
That was the most exciting scene in the play.
scen·er·y
sce·nic
scent (sounds like "cent" and "sent")
That's a lovely scent you're wearing.
scep·ter
sched·ule
sched·ul·ing
scheme
schem·er
schem·ing
schol·ar
schol·ar·ship
school
school yard
schoon·er
sci·ence
sci·en·**tif**·ic
sci·en·tist
scis·sors
scoff
scold
sco·li·**o**·sis

scone
scoop
scoot·er
scope
scorch
score
scor·ing
scorn
scorn·ful
scor·pi·on
scour
scour·er
scourge
scout

scout

scowl
scrag·gi·er
scrag·gi·est
scrag·gy
scram·ble
scram·bled
scram·bler

scram·bling
scrap·book
scrape
scraped
scrap·er
scrap·ing
scrapped
scrap·ping
scratch
scratch·i·er
scratch·i·est
scratch·y
scrawl
scream
screech
screen
screw
screw·driv·er
scrib·ble
scrib·bling
scribe
scrim·mage
script
scrip·ture
script·writ·er
scroll
scrounge
scroung·ing
scrub
scrubbed
scrub·bing
scruff·i·er
scruff·i·est
scruff·y

scru•ple
scru•ples
scru•pu•lous
scru•ti•nize
scru•ti•niz•ing
scru•ti•ny
scu•ba
scuff
scuf•fle
scull
sculpt
sculp•tor
sculp•ture
scum
scur•ried
scur•ries
scur•ry
scur•vy
sea (sounds like "see")
  The ship was lost at sea.
sea a•nem•o•ne
sea•board
sea•far•ing
sea•food
sea•gull
sea horse
seal
sea lev•el
sea li•on
seam (sounds like "seem")
  She ripped the seam of her dress.
seam•stress

sea•plane
sea•port
search
search•er
search•ing
search•light
sea•shell
sea•shore
sea•sick
sea•son
sea•son•al
sea•soned
sea•soning
seat
seat belt
sea ur•chin
sea•weed
se•cede
se•ced•ed
se•ces•sion
se•clud•ed
se•cond
sec•on•dar•y
sec•ond•hand
sec•ond-rate
se•cre•cy
se•cret
sec•re•tar•i•al
sec•re•tar•ies
sec•re•tar•y
se•crete
se•cre•tive
  also pronounced
  se•cre•tive

sec•tion
sec•tor
se•cure
se•cur•ing
se•cu•ri•ties
se•cu•ri•ty
se•dan
se•date
se•dat•ing
se•da•tion
sed•a•tive
sed•i•ment
sed•i•men•tary
sed•i•men•ta•tion
see (sounds like "sea")
  Can you see the parade from here?
seed
seed•ling
seek
seem (sounds like "seam")
  You seem to be in a happy mood today.
seen (sounds like "scene")
  The president was seen on television.
seep
see•saw
seethe
seeth•ing
seg•ment
seg•men•tal

seg•re•gate
seg•re•gat•ing
seg•re•**ga**•tion
seis•mo•graph
seize
seiz•ing
sei•zure
sel•dom
se•**lect**
se•**lec**•tion
se•**lec**•tive
se•**lec**•tor
self
self-**cen**•tered
self-**con**•fi•dence
self-**con**•fi•dent
self-**con**•scious
self-con•**trol**
self-con•**trolled**
self-de•**fense**
self-de•**struct**
self-de•**struc**•tion
self-de•**struc**•tive
self-em•**ployed**
self-em•**ploy**•ment
self-es•**teem**
self-ex•**plan**•a•tory
self•ish
self•ish•ness
self-re•**spect**
self-re•**spect**•ing
self-**serv**•ice
self-**start**•er
self-suf•**fi**•cien•cy

self-suf•**fi**•cient
sell (sounds like "cell")

Did he sell you his bike?

sel•ler
se•**mes**•ter
sem•i•cir•cle
sem•i•**cir**•cu•lar
sem•i•co•lon
sem•i•con•**duc**•tor
sem•i•fi•nal
sem•i•nar•ies
sem•i•nar•y
Sem•i•nole
sen•ate
sen•a•tor
send
send-off
se•nile
se•**nil**•i•ty
sen•ior
sen•ior **cit**•i•zen
sen•**ior**•i•ty
sen•**sa**•tion
sen•**sa**•tion•al
sense
sense•less
sen•si•ble
sen•si•bly
sens•ing
sen•si•tive
sen•si•**tiv**•i•ty
sen•sor

sent (sounds like "cent" and "scent")

She sent me a birthday present.

sen•tence
sen•ti•ment
sen•ti•**ment**•al
sen•ti•ment•**al**•i•ty
sep•a•rate
sep•a•rat•ing
sep•a•**ra**•tion
Sep•**tem**•ber
se•quel
se•quence
se•**quen**•tial
se•**quoi**•a
ser•en•**dip**•i•tous
ser•en•**dip**•i•ty
se•**rene**
se•**ren**•i•ty
serf (sounds like "surf")

The serf worked on the lord's land.

serf•dom
ser•geant
se•ri•al (sounds like "cereal")

Her book was made into a TV serial.

se•ri•a•li•**za**•tion
se•ri•a•lize
se•ri•al **num**•ber
se•ries
se•ri•ous

se•ri•ous•ness
ser•mon
ser•pent
se•rum
serv•ant
serve
serv•er
serv•ice
serv•ic•ing
ses•a•me
ses•sion
set
set•back
set•**tee**
set•ting
set•tle
set•tle•ment
set•tling
set•up
sev•en
sev•enth
sev•er
sev•er•al
se•**vere**
se•**ver**•i•ty
sew (sounds like "so" and "sow")

I have to sew this button on.

sew•age
sew•er
sew•ing ma•**chine**
sex
sex•ism

sex•ist
shab•bi•ly
shab•by
shack
shade
shad•ing
shad•ow
shag•gi•er
shag•gi•est
shag•gy
shake
shak•en
shak•i•er
shak•i•est
shak•ing
shak•y
shall
shal•low
sham•bles
shame
sham•poo
sham•rock
shape
shape•less
shap•ing
share
share•ware
shar•ing
shark
sharp
shat•ter
shave
shav•ing
shawl

Shaw•**nee**
she
sheaf
shear (sounds like "sheer")

Use these clippers to shear the hedge.

shears
sheath
shed
she'd
sheen
sheep
sheep•dog
sheep•ish
sheer (sounds like "shear")

Mom hung sheer curtains in the kitchen.

sheet

shark

sheik (*or* sheikh)

shelf

shell

she'll

shel•**lac**

shel•ter

shelve

shelves

shelv•ing

shep•herd

sher•bet (*or* sher•bert)

sher•iff

sher•iffs

sher•ry

she's

Shet•land **po**•ny

shied

shield

shi•er (*or* **shy**•er)

shies

shi•est (*or* **shy**•est)

shift

shim•mer

shin

shine

shin•gle

shin•gling

shin•ing

shin•ning

Shin•to

shi•ny

ship

ship•ment

shipped

ship•ping

ship•shape

ship•wreck

ship•yard

shirk

shirt

shish ka•bob (*or* **shish** ke•bob)

shiv•er

shiv•er•y

shoal

shock

shod•di•er

shod•di•est

shod•dy

shoe

shoe•horn

shoe•lace

(**ship**)

shoes

shone (sounds like "shown")

The sun shone all day.

shook

shoot (sounds like "chute")

They're going to shoot a movie in our house!

shoot•ing **star**

shop

shop•keeper

shop•lift•er

shopped

shop•ping

shop•ping **cen**•ter

shore

short

short•age

short•bread

short **cir**•cuit

short•com•ing

short•en

short•en•ing

short•hand

short•**hand**•ed

short•ly

short-range

short•sight•ed

short•sight•ed•ness

short•stop

short-temp•ered

shot

shot•gun

shot put

should

shoul•der

shoul•der blade

should•n't

should•'ve

shout

shove

shov•el

shov•ing

show

show busi•ness

show•er

show•er•y

shown (sounds like "shone")

I have shown him around.

show-off

show•room

show•y

shrank

shrap•nel

shred

shred•ded

shred•der

shred•ding

shrewd

shriek

shrill

shrimp

shrine

shrink

shriv•el

shrub

shrub•ber•y

shrug

shrugged

shrug•ging

shrunk

shrunk•en

shud•der

shuf•fle

shuf•fled

shuf•fling

shun

shunned

shun•ning

shut

shut•ter

shut•tle

shut•tling

shy

shy•er (*or* shi•er)

shy•est (*or* shi•est)

shy•ness

Si•a•mese

sib•ling

sick

sick•en

sick•le

sick•le-cell a•ne•mi•a

sick•li•er

sick•li•est

sick•ly

sick•ness

side

side•board

side•burns

sid•ed

side ef•fect

side•line

side•show

side•step

side•stepped

side•step•ping

side•track

side•walk

side•ways

sid•ing

siege

si•er•ra

si•es•ta

sieve

sift

sigh

sighed

sight (sounds like "cite" and "site")

Niagara Falls is an awesome sight.

sight•se•er

sign

sig•nal

sig•na•ture

sig•nif•i•cance

sig•nif•i•cant

sig•ni•fy

sig•ni•fy•ing

sign lan•guage

sign•post

Sikh

si•lence

si•lenc•er

si•lent

sil•hou•**ette**

sil•i•con

silk

silk•y

sil•li•er

sil•li•est

sil•li•ness

sil•ly

si•lo

silt

sil•ver

sil•ver•smith

sil•ver•ware

sil•ver•y

sim•i•lar

sim•i•**lar**•i•ties

sim•i•**lar**•i•ty

sim•i•le

sim•mer

sim•ple

sim•pler

sim•plest

sim•**plic**•i•ty

sim•pli•fi•**ca**•tion

sim•pli•fied

sim•pli•fies

sim•pli•fy

sim•ply

sim•u•late

sim•u•lat•ing

sim•u•**la**•tion

sim•u•la•tor

si•mul•**ta**•ne•ous

sin

since

sin•**cere**

sin•**cere**•ly

sin•**cer**•i•ty

sing

sin•gle

sin•gle-**hand**•ed

sin•gle-**mind**•ed

sin•gu•lar

sin•i•ster

sink

sinned

sin•ner

sin•ning

si•nus

Sioux (sounds like "sue")

The Sioux inhabited the northern Great Plains.

sip

sipped

sip•ping

sir

si•ren

sis•ter

sis•ter•hood

sis•ter-in-law

sis•ters-in-law

sit

sit•com

site (sounds like "cite" and "sight")

This is a perfect site for our house.

sit•ting

sit•u•ate

sit•u•at•ing

sit•u•**a**•tion

sit-up

six

sixth

siz•a•ble (*or* size•a•ble)

size

siz•zle

siz•zling

skate

skate•board

skel•e•ton

skep•tic

skep•ti•cal

sketch

sketch•y

skew•er

ski

skid

skid•ded

skid•ding

skied

skies

ski•ing

skill

skilled

skil•let

skill•ful

skim
skim milk
skin
skinned
skin•ni•er
skin•ni•est
skin•ni•ness
skin•ning
skin•ny
skip
skipped
skip•ping
skirt
skit
skit•tish
skull
skunk
sky
sky•box
sky•dive
sky•div•er
sky•div•ing
sky•lark
sky•light
sky•line
sky•rock•et
sky•scrap•er
slab
slack
slain
sla•lom
slam
slammed
slam•ming

sledding

slan•der
slan•der•ous
slang
slant
slap
slap•dash
slapped
slap•ping
slap•stick
slash
slat
slate
slaugh•ter
slave
slav•ing
slay (sounds like
   "sleigh")
   *How did David slay
   Goliath?*
sled
sled•ded

sled•ding
sledge•ham•mer
sleek
sleep
sleep•i•er
sleep•i•est
sleep•i•ness
sleep•ing **bag**
sleep•walk•er
sleepy
sleet
sleeve
sleigh (sounds like
   "slay")
   *It's snowing, so hitch
   up the sleigh.*
sleight (sounds like
   "slight")
   *The tricks involved
   sleight of hand.*
slen•der
slept
sleuth
slew
slice
slic•ing
slick
slid
slide
slid•ing
slight (sounds like
   "sleight")
   *There is a slight
   chance of rain.*

slim
slime
slimmed
slim•ming
sling
sling•shot
slip
slipped
slip•per
slip•per•y
slip•ping
slip•shod
slit
slith•er
sliv•er
slo•gan
sloop
slop
slope
slop•ing
slopped
slop•ping
slop•py
slosh
slot
sloth
slouch
slov•en•ly
slow
slow•ly
sludge
slug
slugged
slug•ging

slug•gish
slug•gish•ness
slum
slum•ber
slump
slur
slurp
slurred
slur•ring
slush
sly
smack
small
small•pox
smart
smart•ness
smash
smear
smell
smell•y
smile
smil•ing
smirk
smock
smog
smoke
smoke a•larm
smoke de•tec•tor
smoke•stack
smok•y
smol•der
smooth
smooth•ness
smoth•er

smudge
smudg•ing
smug
smug•gle
snack
snag
snagged
snag•ging
snail
snake
snak•ing
snap
snap•drag•on
snap•shot
snare drum
snatch
sneak
sneak•ers
sneak•i•ly
sneer

smokestack

sneeze
sneez•ing
snick•er
sniff
snif•fle
snip
snipe
snip•er
snip•ing
snipped
snip•ping
snob
snob•ber•y
snoop
snoop•y
snoot•y
snooze
snooz•ing
snore
snor•ing
snor•kel
snort
snout
snow
snow•ball
snow•flake
snow•mo•bile
snow•plow
snow•shoe
snow•storm
snow•y
snub
snubbed
snub•bing

snuff
snuf•fle
snuf•fling
snug
snug•ger
snug•gest
snug•gle
snug•gled
snug•gling
snug•gly
  (often confused
  with "snugly")
  *The teddy bear was
  soft and snuggly.*
snug•ly
  (often confused
  with "snuggly")
  The dress fit snugly.
so (sounds like "sew"
  and "sow")
  *He was so tired after
  the race, he fell
  asleep.*
soak
soak•ing
soap
soap op•er•a
soar
sob
sobbed
sob•bing
so•ber
soc•cer
so•cia•ble
so•cia•**bil**•i•ty

so•cia•bly
so•cial
so•cial•ism
so•cial•ly
So•cial Se•**cu**•ri•ty
so•cial **stud**•ies
so•**ci**•e•ties
so•**ci**•e•ty
so•ci•o•**log**•i•cal
so•ci•**ol**•o•gist
so•ci•**ol**•o•gy
sock
sock•et
sod
so•da
so•da **foun**•tain
so•da **wa**•ter
sod•den
sod•ding
so•di•um
so•di•um
  bi•**car**•bon•ate
so•fa
soft
soft•ball
soft drink
soft•heart•ed
soft•ness
soft•ware
sog•gi•er
sog•gi•est
sog•**gy**
soil
sol•ace

so•lar

so•lar **en**•er•gy

so•lar **sys**•tem

sold

sol•dier

sole (sounds like "soul")

  Tom was the sole survivor.

sol•emn

sol•em•ness

sol•id

sol•i•**dar**•i•ty

so•**lid**•i•fy

sol•id•ly

sol•i•tar•y

sol•i•tar•y con•**fine**•ment

so•lo

so•loed

so•lo•ing

so•los

sol•u•ble

so•**lu**•tion

solve

sol•vent

solv•er

solv•ing

som•ber

som•**bre**•ro

som•**bre**•ros

some

some•bod•y

some•day

some•how

some•one

som•er•sault

some•thing

some•time

some•times

some•what

some•where

son (sounds like "sun")

  His son left for college this fall.

so•nar

so•**na**•ta

song

son•ic

son•ic **boom**

son-in-law

son•net

sons-in-law

soon

soot

soothe

sooth•ing

so•**phis**•ti•ca•ted

so•**phis**•ti•**ca**•tion

Soph•o•cles

soph•o•more

sop•ping

so•**pran**•o

so•**pran**•os

sor•**bet**

  also pronounced **sor**•bet

sor•cer•er

sor•cer•y

sor•did

sor•did•ness

sore

sore•ness

sor•ri•er

sor•ri•est

sor•row

sor•row•ful

sor•ry

sort

sought

soul (sounds like "sole")

  I love you to the bottom of my soul.

sound

sound•proof

soup

sour

source

sour•dough

south

South Car•o•**li**•na

South Da•**ko**•ta

South•**east**

south•ern

South•ern Hem•i•sphere

South Pole

South•**west**

sou•ve•**nir**

  also pronounced **sou**•ve•nir

sov•er•eign

So•vi•et **Un**•ion

sow (sounds like "sew" and "so")

The farmer must sow his seeds.

sow (rhymes with "cow")

The sow gave birth to eight piglets.

soy•bean

soy sauce

space

space bar

space•craft

space•ship

space•suit

space•walk

spac•ing

spa•cious

spade

spa•**ghet**•ti

span

spank

spanned

span•ning

spare

spar•ing

spark

spar•kle

spark•ling

spark plug

spar•row

sparse

spas•m

spat

spat•ter

spat•u•la

spawn

speak

speak•er

spear

spear•mint

spe•cial

spe•cial•ist

spe•cial•ize

spe•cial•iz•ing

spe•cial•ties

spacesuit

spe•cial•ty

spe•cies

spe•**ci**•fic

spe•**ci**•fi•cal•ly

spe•ci•fi•**ca**•tions

spec•i•fied

spec•i•fies

spec•i•fy

spec•i•fy•ing

spec•i•men

speck

speck•led

spec•ta•cle

spec•**tac**•u•lar

spec•ta•tor

spec•ter

spec•tral

spec•trum

spec•u•late

spec•u•lat•ing

spec•u•**la**•tion

speech

speech•less

speed

speed bump

speed•**om**•e•ter

spell

spell check•er

spe•**lunk**•ing

spend

sperm

sphere

spher•i•cal

sphinx

spice

spi•cy

spi•der

spied

spies

spike
spik•ing
spill
spin
spin•ach
spi•nal
spi•nal **cord**
spin•dle
spind•ly
spine
spin•ning
spin•ning **wheel**
spin-off
spin•ster
spin•y
spi•ral
spire
spir•it
spir•i•tu•al
spit
spite
spit•ting
splash
splash•down
splat•ter
splen•did
splen•dor
splint
splin•ter
split
split•ting
spoil
spoke
spok•en

sponge
spong•y
spon•sor
spon•sor•ship
spon•ta•**ne**•i•ty
spon•**ta**•ne•ous
spool
spoon
spore
sport
sports•man•ship
spot
spot•less
spot•light
spot•ted

spotted

spot•ting
spouse
spout
sprain
sprang
sprawl

spray
spread
spree
spring
spring•board
spring-
   clean•ing
spring•time
sprin•kle
sprin•kler
sprink•ling
sprint
sprout
spruce
sprung
spun
spur
spurt
sput•ter
spy
spy•ing
squab•ble
squab•bling
squad
squad•ron
squan•der
square
square dance
square root
squash
squat•ter
squawk
squeak
squeal

squea·mish
squeez·a·ble
squeeze
squeez·ing
squid
squig·gle
squinch
squint
squire
squirm
squir·rel
squirt
squish·y
stab
stabbed
stab·bing
sta·bi·lize
sta·ble
stac·ca·to
stack
sta·di·um
staff
stag
stage
stage·coach
stag·ger
stag·ger·ing
stag·ing
stag·nant
stag·na·tion
staid
stain
stained glass
stain·less **steel**

stair (sounds like
  "stare")
*She tripped on the
stair and fell.*
stair·way
stake (sounds like
  "steak")
*Use this stake to set
up the tent.*
stak·ing
sta·**lac**·tite
sta·**lag**·mite
stale
stale·mate
stalk
stall
stal·lion
sta·men
stam·i·na
stam·mer
stamp
stam·**pede**
stam·**ped**·ing
stand
stan·dard
stand·by
stand-in
stand·ing
stand·still
stand-up
stank
stan·za
sta·ple
star

star·board
starch
star·dom
star·dust
stare (sounds like
  "stair")
*You shouldn't stare
at people.*
stared
star·fish
star·gaz·er
star·ing
stark
star·less
star·light
star·ling
star·ry-eyed
star-spang·led
star-stud·ded
start
star·tle
start·ling
star·**va**·tion
starve
starv·ing
state
state·ly
state·ment
state-of-the-art
stat·ic
stat·ic
  e·lec·**tric**·i·ty
stat·ing
sta·tion

sta•tion•ar•y (sounds like "stationery")

The stationary target was easy to hit.

sta•tion•er•y (sounds like "stationary")

I'll buy envelopes at the stationery store.

sta•tion **wag**•on

sta•**tis**•tic

sta•tus

stay

stead•fast

stead•i•ly

stead•y

steak (sounds like "stake")

He likes to eat steak.

steal (sounds like "steel")

Did your brother steal your wallet?

stealth

stealth•y

steam

steam•boat

steam en•gine

steam•rol•ler

steam•ship

steed

steel (sounds like "steal")

The bridge is made of steel.

steel wool

steep

stee•ple

steer

steer•ing

steg•o•**sau**•rus

stel•lar

stem

stemmed

stem•ming

stench

sten•cil

step (sounds like "steppe")

Step right up, ladies and gentlemen.

step•fami•lies

step•fami•ly

step•fa•ther

step•moth•er

steppe (sounds like "step")

A steppe is a vast, grassy plain.

stepped

step•ping

ste•re•o

ste•r•eos

ster•e•o•type

ster•ile

ster•il•i•**za**•tion

ster•i•lize

ster•ling

stern

ste•roid

steth•o•scope

stew

stew•ard

stew•ard•ess

stick

stick•er

sties (or **styes**)

stiff

stif•fen

sti•fle

sti•fling

stig•ma

stig•ma•tize

still

stilt

stim•u•lant

stim•u•late

stim•u•lat•ing

stim•u•**la**•tion

stim•u•lus

sting

sting•er

sting•ray

stin•gy

stink

stir

stir-fried

stir-fries

stir-fry

stirred

stir•ring

stir•rup

stitch

stock

stock•**ade**
stock•bro•ker
stock car
stock•hold•er
Stock•holm
stock•ing
stock•pile
stocks
stock•y
stock•yard
stodg•i•er
stodg•i•est
stodg•y
sto•ic
stoke
stok•ing
stole
sto•len
stom•ach
stom•ach•ache
stomp
stone
stone•wall
stone•washed
stood
stool
stoop
stop
stop•light
stopped
stop•per
stop•ping
stop•watch
stor•age

store
store•keep•er
sto•ries
stor•ing
stork

stork

storm
sto•ry
stout
stove
stow
stow•a•way
strag•**gle**
strag•gler
strag•gling
straight (sounds like "strait")
She rushed straight home after work.
straight•en

strain
strait (sounds like "straight")
We sailed quickly through the strait.
strand
strange
strange•ly
strange•ness
strang•er
strang•est
stran•gle
stran•gler
stran•gling
stran•gu•**la**•tion
strap
strapped
strap•ping
strat•e•gies
strat•e•gist
strat•e•gy
strat•o•sphere
straw
straw•ber•ries
straw•ber•ry
stray
streak
streak•y
stream
stream•er
stream•lined
street
street•light
street•wise

strength
strength•en
stren•u•ous
stress
stress•ful
stretch
strict
stride
strid•ing
strife
strike
strik•er
strik•ing
string
string bean
strings
strip
stripped
strip•ping
stripe
strive
striv•en
striv•ing
strobe
stroke
stroll
strong
strong•hold
struc•ture
strug•gle
strug•gling
strum
strummed
strut

strut•ted
stub
stubbed
stub•bing
stub•born
stuck
stuck-up
stu•dent
stud•ied
stud•ies
stu•di•o
stu•di•os
stu•di•ous
stud•y
stud•y•ing
stuff
stuf•fing
stuf•fy
stum•ble
stum•bling
stump
stump•y
stun
stunk
stunned
stun•ning
stunt
stu•pen•dous
stu•pid
stu•pid•i•ty
stur•dy
stut•ter
stut•ter•er
sty

styes (or sties)
style
sty•ling
sty•lish
sty•list
Sty•ro•foam
sub•con•scious
sub•con•ti•nent
sub•di•vide
   also pronounced
   sub•di•vide
sub•di•vi•sion
   also pronounced
   sub•di•vi•sion
sub•ject (n.)
sub•ject (v.)
sub•ma•rine
   also pronounced
   sub•ma•rine
sub•merge
sub•mit
sub•mit•ted
sub•mit•ting
sub•scribe
sub•scrib•er
sub•scrib•ing
sub•scrip•tion
sub•se•quent
sub•set
sub•si•dies
sub•si•dize
sub•si•dy
sub•stance
sub•stan•tial

sub•sti•tute
sub•sti•**tu**•tion
sub•ter•**ra**•ne•an
sub•ti•tle
sub•tle
sub•tle•ty
sub•**tract**
sub•**trac**•tion
sub•tra•hend
sub•**trop**•ics
sub•urb
sub•**ur**•ban
sub•**ur**•ban•ite
sub•**ur**•bi•a
sub•way
suc•**ceed**
suc•**cess**
suc•**cess**•ful
suc•cu•lent
such
suck
suck•er
suc•tion
sud•den
sud•den•ness
suds
sue (sounds like "Sioux")

She's going to sue him in court.

suede
suf•fer
suf•**fi**•cient
suf•fix

suf•fo•cate
suf•fo•cat•ing
suf•fo•**ca**•tion
suf•frage
sug•ar

sugar

sug•ar•y
sug•**gest**
sug•**gest**•ion
su•i•**ci**•dal
su•i•cide
su•ing
suit
suit•a•**bil**•i•ty
suit•a•ble
suit•a•bly
suit•case
suite (sounds like "sweet")

We had a big suite at the hotel.

sul•fur
sul•fur di•**ox**•ide
sulk
sulk•y
sul•len
sul•tan
sul•try
sum
su•mac
sum•ma•ries
sum•ma•rize
sum•ma•ry (sounds like "summery")

Write a summary of the book.

sum•**ma**•tion
summed
sum•mer
sum•mer•time
sum•mer•y (sounds like "summary")

It was a warm, summery day.

sum•ming
sum•mit
sum•mon
sum•mons
su•mo **wres**•tling
sun (sounds like "son")

The sun is over 90 million miles from Earth.

sun•bath (n.)
sun•bathe (v.)

sun·burn

sun·dae (sounds like "Sunday")

Have an ice-cream sundae.

Sun·day (sounds like "sundae")

Sunday comes before Monday.

sun·dial

sun·down

sun·flow·er

sun·glass·es

sunk

sunk·en

sun·light

sun·ny

sun·rise

sun·screen

sun·set

sun·shine

sun·stroke

sun·tan

su·per

su·perb

su·per·fi·cial

su·per·her·o

su·per·hu·man

su·per·im·pose

su·per·in·ten·dent

su·pe·ri·or

su·pe·ri·or·i·ty

su·per·la·tive

su·per·mar·ket

su·per·nat·u·ral

su·per·no·va

su·per·pow·er

su·per·son·ic

su·per·sti·tion

su·per·sti·tious

su·per·tank·er

su·per·vise

su·per·vis·ing

su·per·vi·sion

su·per·vi·sor

sup·per

sup·ple

sup·ple·ment

sup·ple·men·ta·ry

sup·plied

sup·pli·er

sup·plies

sup·ply

sup·ply·ing

sup·port

sup·port·er

sup·port·ive

sup·pose

su·preme

sure

sure·ly

surf (sounds like "serf")

Surf's up!

sur·face

sur·fac·ing

surf·board

surf·er

surge

sur·geon

sur·ger·y

sur·gi·cal

sur·li·ness

sur·ly

sur·pass

sur·plus

sur·prise

sur·pris·ing

sur·ren·der

sur·round

sur·round·ings

sur·vey (v.)

sur·vey (n.)

sur·viv·al

sur·vive

sur·viv·ing

sur·vi·vor

sus·pect (v.)

sus·pect (n.)

sus·pend

sus·pend·ers

sus·pense

sus·pen·sion

sus·pi·cion

sus·pi·cious

swag·ger

swal·low

swam

swamp

swamp·y

swan

swap

swapped

swap•ping
swarm
swarth•y
swas•ti•ka
swat
swat•ted
swat•ting
sway
swear
sweat
sweat•er
sweat•shirt
sweep
sweep•ing
sweet (sounds like "suite")

This candy is sweet.

sweet•en
sweet•heart
swell
swel•ter
swel•ter•ing
swept
swerve
swerv•ing
swift
swift•ness
swig
swigged
swig•ging
swim
swim•mer
swim•ming
swim•suit

swin•dle
swin•dler
swin•dling
swine
swing
swipe
swip•ing
swirl
swish
switch
switch•board
swiv•el
swol•len
swoon
swoop
sword
sword•fish
swore
sworn
swum
swung

swelter

syc•a•more
syl•la•ble
syl•la•bus
sym•bol (sounds like "cymbal")

The Statue of Liberty is a symbol of freedom.

sym•bol•ize
sym•**met**•ri•cal
sym•me•try
sym•pa•thize
sym•pa•thy
sym•**phon**•ic
sym•pho•nies
sym•pho•ny
symp•tom
syn•a•gogue
syn•chro•nize
syn•co•pate
syn•drome
syn•o•nym
syn•**op**•ses (pl.)
syn•**op**•sis (sing.)
syn•the•size
syn•the•siz•er
syn•**thet**•ic
sy•phon
Syr•i•a
sy•**ringe**
syr•up
sys•tem
sys•tem•**at**•ic
sys•tem•**at**•i•cal•ly

185

tab

tabbed

tab•bing

tab•by

tab•er•na•cle

ta•ble

ta•ble•cloth

ta•ble•spoon

tab•let

ta•ble ten•nis

tab•loid

ta•boo

tab•u•late

tab•u•lat•ing

tab•u•la•tion

tack

tack•le

ta•co

ta•cos

tact

tact•ful

tac•ti•cal

tac•tics

tad•pole

taf•fy

tag

tagged

tag•ging

tail (sounds like "tale")

The dog wags its tail when it's happy.

tail•gate

tail•gat•ing

tai•lor

take

take•off

take•out

tambourine

take•o•ver

tak•ing

tal•cum pow•der

tale (sounds like "tail")

He told me an exciting tale of adventure.

tal•ent

talk

talk•a•tive

tall

tal•lied

tal•lies

tal•ly

Tal•mud

tal•on

ta•ma•le

tam•bou•rine

tame

tam•per

tan

tan•dem

tan•door•i

tan•ge•lo

tan•gent

tan•ger•ine

tan•gle

tan•gling

tan•gram

tang•y

tank

tank•er

tanned

tan•ner•y

tan•ning

tan•trum

tap

tap danc•ing

tape

taped

tape meas•ure

ta•per

tape re•cord•er

tap•es•try

tap•ing

tapped

tap•ping

taps
tar
ta•**ran**•tu•la
tar•di•ness
tar•dy
tar•get
tar•iff
tar•nish
tar•pau•lin
tarred
tar•ring
tart
tar•tan
tar•tar
task
tas•sel
taste
taste bud
taste•less
tast•ing
tat•tered
tat•tle
tat•tler
tat•tle•tale
tat•tling
tat•too
taught
taunt
tav•ern
tax
tax•**a**•tion
tax•i
tax•i•cab
tax•ied

tax•ies (v.)
tax•i•ing
tax•is (pl. n.)
tea
teach
teach•er
tea•ket•tle
teal
team (sounds like "teem")
  I made the football team!
team•mate
tear (sounds like "tier")
  I cried many a tear.
tear (rhymes with "hare")
  Don't tear the magazine.
tease
teased
teas•ing
tea•spoon
tea•spoon•ful
tech•ni•cal
tech•**ni**•cian
tech•**nique**
tech•no•**log**•i•cal
tech•**nol**•o•gies
tech•**nol**•o•gy
ted•dy **bear**
te•di•ous
teem (sounds like "team")

  The city streets teem with people.
teen•age (*or* **teen**-age)
teen•aged (*or* **teen**-aged)
teen•ag•er (*or* **teen**-ag•er)
teens
tee•pee (*or* **te**•pee)
tee shirt (*or* **T**-shirt)
teeth
teethe
teeth•ing
Tef•lon
tel•e•cast
tel•e•com•mu•ni•**ca**•tion
tel•e•com•**mute**
tel•e•com•**mut**•er
tel•e•com•**mut**•ing
tel•e•gram
tel•e•graph
tel•e•graph•er
tel•e•mar•ket•ing
tel•e•phone
tel•e•phon•ing
tel•e•**pho**•to **lens**
tel•e•scope
tel•e•**scop**•ic
tel•e•thon
tel•e•vise
tel•e•vis•ing
tel•e•vi•sion
tell

tel•ler
tem•per
tem•per•a•ment
tem•per•a•**men**•tal
tem•per•ate
tem•per•a•ture
tem•pest
tem•plate
tem•ple
tem•po
tem•po•**rar**•i•ly
tem•po•rar•y
tem•pos
tempt
temp•**ta**•tion
tempt•er
ten
ten•ant
tend
ten•den•cies
ten•den•cy
ten•der
ten•der•ness
ten•don
ten•e•ment
Ten•nes•**see**
  also pronounced
  Ten•nes•see
ten•nis
ten•or
tense (sounds like
  "tents")
  Try not to get tense.
ten•sion

tent
ten•ta•cle
ten•ta•tive
ten•ter•hooks
tenth
tents (sounds like
  "tense")
  *How many tents
  were in the camp?*
ten•u•ous
te•pee (*or* tee•pee)
tep•id
ter•i•**ya**•ki
term
ter•mi•nal
ter•mi•nate
ter•mi•nat•ing
ter•mite
ter•race
ter•ra-**cot**•ta
ter•**rain**
ter•ra•pin
ter•**rar**•i•um
ter•**res**•tri•al
ter•ri•ble
ter•ri•bly
ter•ri•er
ter•**ri**•fic
ter•ri•fied
ter•ri•fies
ter•ri•fy
ter•ri•fy•ing
ter•ri•**to**•ri•al
ter•ri•to•ries

ter•ri•to•ry
ter•ror
ter•ror•ist
ter•ror•ize
ter•ror•iz•ing
terse
test
tes•ta•ment
test•i•fied
test•i•fies
test•i•fy
test•i•fy•ing
tes•ti•mo•ny
test tube
tet•a•nus
teth•er
Tex•as
Tex-Mex
text
text•book
tex•tile
tex•ture
than
thank
thank•ful
thank•less
Thanks•**giv**•ing **Day**
that
thatch
that's
thaw
the
the•a•ter (*or* **the**•a•tre)
the•**at**•ri•cal

thee

theft

their (sounds like
"there" and "they're")
This is their house.

theirs

them

theme

them•**selves**

then

the•o•**log**•i•cal

the•**ol**•o•gy

the•o•rem

the•o•**ret**•i•cal

the•o•ries

the•o•ry

ther•a•pies

ther•a•pist

ther•a•py

there (sounds like
"their" and "they're")
*There are the books I
was looking for.*

there•**af**•ter

there•by
also pronounced
there•**by**

there•fore

there's

therm

ther•mal

ther•**mom**•e•ter

ther•mos **bot**•tle

ther•mo•stat

the•**sau**•rus

these

they

they'd

they'll

they're (sounds like
"their" and "there")
*They're coming here
on Sunday.*

they've

thick

thief

thief

thieves

thigh

thim•ble

thin

thing

think

thin•ness

third

thirst

thirst•i•er

thirst•i•est

thirst•y

this

this•tle

thong

tho•rax

thorn

thorn•i•er

thorn•i•est

thorn•y

thor•ough

thor•ough•fare

thor•ough•ness

those

thou

though

thought

thought•ful

thought•less

thou•sand

thou•sandth

thrash

thread

thread•bare

threat

threat•en

three

three-di•men•sion•al

thresh

thresh•old

threw (sounds like
"through")
*She threw the ball
to the catcher.*

thrift•i•er

thrift•i•est

thrift•i•ness

thrift•y

thrill

thril•ler

thril•ling

thrive

thriv•ing

throat

throb

throne (sounds like "thrown")

The dizzy king fell off his throne.

throng

throt•tle

throt•tling

through (sounds like "threw")

The ball flew right through the window.

through•out

through•way (*or* thru•way)

throw

thrown (sounds like "throne")

My homework was thrown away!

thud

thug

thumb

thumb•tack

thump

thun•der

thun•der•storm

Thurs•day

thus

thwart

thy

thyme (sounds like "time")

Season the food with a little thyme.

ti•ar•a

tick

tick•et

tick•le

tick•ling

tick•lish

tick-tack-toe (*or* tic-tac-toe)

tid•al

tid•al **wave**

tid•bit

tid•dle•dy•winks (*or* tid•dly•winks)

tide

ti•di•er

ti•di•est

ti•di•ness

tid•ings

ti•dy

tie

tie•break•er

tied

tier (sounds like "tear")

Our theater seats were in the first tier.

ties

ti•ger

(**tiger**)

ti•ger li•ly

tight

tight•rope

tights

tile

till

till•er

tilt

tim•ber

tim•ber•line

time (sounds like "thyme")

What time does the show begin?

time•keep•er

time•less

time•ly

time-out

time·piece

time·sav·er

time·ta·ble

time·worn

time zone

tim·id

ti·**mid**·i·ty

tim·id·ness

tin

tinge

tin·gle

tin·gling

ti·ni·er

ti·ni·est

ti·ni·ness

tin·ker

tin·kle

tin·kling

tint

ti·ny

tip

tipped

tip·ping

tip·toe

tire

tired·ness

tire·less

tire·some

tir·ing

tis·sue

ti·tle

Tlin·git

to (sounds like "too" and "two")

I'm going to the store.

toad (sounds like "towed")

She caught a toad in the pond.

toad·stool

toast

toast·er

to·**bac**·co

to·**bog**·gan

to·**day**

tod·dle

tod·dler

toe (sounds like "tow")

What color did you paint your big toe?

tof·fee

to·fu

to·ga

to·**geth**·er

toil

toil·er

toi·let

to·ken

told

tol·er·ance

tol·er·ant

tol·er·ate

tol·er·at·ing

tol·er·**a**·tion

toll

tom·a·hawk

to·**ma**·to

to·**ma**·toes

tomb

tom·boy

tomb·stone

tom·cat

to·**mor**·row

ton

tone

tongs

tongue

tongue twist·er

ton·ic

to·**night**

ton·sil·**li**·tis

ton·sils

too (sounds like "to" and "two")

It's too hot to dance.

took

tool

tool·box

toot

tooth

tooth·ache

tooth·brush

tooth·paste

tooth·pick

top

to·paz

top·ic

top·i·cal

top·o·**graph**·i·cal

to·**pog**·ra·phy

topped

top·ping

top·ple
top·pling
top·soil
top·sy-**tur**·vy
To·rah
torch
to·re·a·dor
tor·ment (n.)
tor·**ment** (v.)
tor·**men**·tor
tor·**na**·do
tor·**na**·does (*or*
  tor·**na**·dos)
tor·**pe**·do
tor·**pe**·does
tor·rent
tor·rid
tor·so
tor·**til**·la
tor·toise
tor·ture
tor·tur·ing
toss
tot
to·tal
tote
to·tem **pole**
tot·ing
tot·ter
tou·can
touch
touch·down
touch·i·er
touch·i·est

touch·ing
touch·y
tough
tou·**pee**
tour
tour·ism
tour·ist
tour·na·ment
tour·ni·quet
tout
tow (sounds like "toe")
*The tow truck took
my car away.*
toward
  also pronounced
    to·**ward**
towards
  also pronounced
    to·**wards**
towed (sounds like
  "toad")
*My car was towed to
the garage.*
tow·el
tow·er
town
tox·ic
toy
trace
trac·ing
track
tract
trac·tion
trac·tor

trade
trad·ed
trade·mark
trad·er
trad·ing
trad·ing **post**
tra·**di**·tion
traf·fic
traf·ficked
traf·ficking
traf·fic **light**
trag·e·dies
trag·e·dy
trag·ic
trail
trail bike
trail·er
train
train·er
trait
trai·tor
tramp
tram·ple
tram·pling
tram·po·**line**
  also pronounced
    tram·po·line
trance
tran·quil
tran·**quil**·i·ty
tran·quil·ly
trans·**ac**·tion
trans·at·**lan**·tic
trans·con·ti·**nen**·tal

tran•**scribe**
tran•**scrib**•ing
tran•script
tran•**scrip**•tion
trans•**fer**
trans•ferred
trans•**fer**•ring
trans•**form**
trans•for•**ma**•tion
trans•**form**•er
trans•**fu**•sion
tran•sient
tran•**sis**•tor
tran•sit
tran•**si**•tion
tran•si•tive
trans•**late**
  also pronounced
  trans•late
trans•lat•ing
trans•**la**•tion
trans•la•tor
trans•**lu**•cent
trans•**mis**•sion
trans•**mit**
trans•**mit**•ted
trans•**mit**•ter
trans•**mit**•ting
tran•som
trans•**par**•en•cies
trans•**par**•en•cy
trans•**par**•ent
tran•spi•**ra**•tion
tran•**spire**

tran•**spir**•ing
trans•**plant** (v.)
trans•plant (n.)
trans•**port** (v.)
trans•port (n.)
trans•por•**ta**•tion
trap
trap•door
tra•**peze**
trap•e•zoid
trapped
trap•per
trap•ping
trash
trau•ma
trau•**mat**•ic
trav•el
trav•el **a**•gent
trav•el•er
trawl
trawl•er
tray
treach•er•ous
treach•er•y
tread
tread•mill
trea•son
treas•ure
treas•ur•er
treas•u•ry
treat
trea•ties
trea•ty
treb•le

tree
trek
trekked
trek•king
trel•lis
trem•ble
trem•bling
tre•**men**•dous
trem•or
trench
trend
trend•y
tres•pass
tres•pass•er
tres•tle
tri•al

treadmill

tri•an•gle
tri•**an**•gu•lar
tri•**ath**•lon
tri•bal

tribe
trib•u•**la**•tion
tri•**bu**•nal
trib•u•tar•ies
trib•u•tar•y
trib•ute
tri•**ce**•ra•tops
trich•i•**no**•sis
trick
trick•i•er
trick•i•est
trick•i•ness
trick•le
trick•ling
trick or treat (n.)
trick-or-treat (v.)
trick•y
tri•cy•cle
tried
tries
tri•fle
tri•fling
trig•ger
tril•o•gy
trim
trim•ming
trim•mings
tri•o
trip
trip•le
trip•let
tri•pling
tri•pod
tripped

trip•ping
tri•umph
tri•**um**•phant
triv•i•a
triv•i•al
troll
trol•ley
trom•**bone**
troop

trick or treat

troop•er
tro•phies
tro•phy
trop•i•cal
trop•ics
trot
trot•ted
trot•ter

trot•ting
trou•ble
trou•ble•some
trough
trou•sers
trout
tru•an•cy
tru•ant
truce
truck
trudge
trudg•ing
true
tru•ly
trum•pet
trunk
trust
trust•wor•thy
trust•y
truth
truth•ful
try
try•ing
tsar (*or* **czar**)
tsa•**ri**•na (*or* cza•**ri**•na)
T-shirt (*or* **tee** shirt)
tsu•**na**•mi
tub
tu•ba
tube
tu•ber•cu•**lo**•sis
tub•ing
tu•bu•lar
tuck

Tues•day

tug

tugged

tug•ging

tug-of-war

tu•**i**•tion

tu•lip

tum•ble

tum•bler

tum•ble•weed

tum•bling

tum•mies

tum•my

tu•mor

tu•mult

tu•na

tun•dra

tune

tu•nic

tun•ing **fork**

tun•nel

tun•nel **vi**•sion

tur•ban

tur•bine

tur•bo•fan

tur•bu•lent

turf

tur•key

tur•moil

turn

tur•nip

turn•out

turn•pike

turn•stile

turn•ta•ble

tur•pen•tine

tur•quoise

tur•ret

tur•tle

tur•tle•neck

tusk

tus•sle

tus•sling

tu•tor

tu•tu

tux•**e**•do

tux•**e**•dos

tweed

twee•zers

twelfth

twelve

twen•ti•eth

twen•ty

twice

twig

twi•light

twin

twine

twinge

twin•kle

twin•kling

twirl

twist

twis•ter

twitch

twit•ter

two (sounds like "to"
and "too")
*I'll have two
pizzas please.*

ty•**coon**

ty•ing

type

type•set

type•set•ter

type•set•ting

type•writ•er

ty•**phoid**

ty•**phoon**

typ•i•cal

typ•ist

ty•**ran**•ni•cal

ty•**ran**•no•saur

tyr•an•ny

ty•rant

ug·li·er
ug·li·est
ug·ly
u·ku·le·le
ul·cer
ul·ti·mate
ul·ti·ma·tum
ul·tra
ul·tra·light
ul·tra·son·ic
ul·tra·sound
ul·tra·vi·o·let
U·lys·ses
um·bil·i·cal cord
um·brel·la
um·pire
un·a·ble
un·ac·cept·a·ble
un·ac·cus·tomed
un·af·fect·ed
un·aid·ed
u·nan·i·mous
un·ap·proach·a·ble
un·armed
un·au·tho·rized
un·a·void·a·ble
un·a·void·a·bly
un·a·ware
un·bear·a·ble
un·bear·a·bly
un·beat·en
un·be·com·ing

un·be·liev·a·ble
un·be·liev·a·bly
un·bend·ing
un·bi·ased
un·break·a·ble
un·bro·ken
un·bur·den
un·but·ton
un·can·ni·ly
un·can·ny
un·cer·tain
un·cer·tain·ty
un·civ·i·lized
un·cle
un·com·fort·a·ble
un·com·fort·a·bly
un·com·mon
un·com·pro·mis·ing
un·con·cerned
un·con·di·tion·al
un·con·firmed
un·con·scious
un·con·sti·tu·tion·al
un·con·trol·la·ble
un·co·op·er·a·tive
un·couth
un·cov·er
un·daunt·ed
un·de·cid·ed
un·de·ni·able
un·de·ni·a·bly
un·der

un·der·arm
un·der·brush
un·der·clothes
un·der·de·vel·oped
un·der·dog
un·der·es·ti·mate
un·der·foot
un·der·go
un·der·goes
un·der·gone
un·der·ground
Un·der·ground
  Rail·road
un·der·hand
un·der·hand·ed
un·der·line
un·der·lin·ing
un·der·mine
un·der·min·ing
un·der·neath
un·der·pants
un·der·pass
un·der·pop·u·la·ted
un·der·priv·i·leged
un·der·sea
un·der·shirt
un·der·stand
un·der·stand·a·ble
un·der·stand·a·bly
un·der·stand·ing
un·der·stood
un·der·take

un·der·tak·er
un·der·**took**
un·der·tow
un·der·wa·ter
un·der·wear
un·der·weight
un·der·**went**
un·der·world
un·de·**sir**·a·ble
un·dis·**turbed**
un·**do**
un·**done**
un·**dress**
un·**dy**·ing
un·**earth**
un·**eas**·i·ly
un·**eas**·i·ness
un·**eas**·y
un·em·**ployed**
un·em·**ploy**·ment
un·**e**·qual
un·**e**·ven
un·e·**vent**·ful
un·ex·**pect**·ed
un·**fair**
un·**fair**·ly
un·**fair**·ness
un·**faith**·ful
un·fa·**mil**·iar
un·**fas**·ten
un·**feel**·ing
un·**fin**·ish·ed
un·**fit**
un·**fold**

un·fore·**seen**
un·for·**get**·ta·ble
un·for·**giv**·a·ble
un·**for**·tu·nate
un·**for**·tu·nate·ly
un·**friend**·ly
un·**grate**·ful
un·**hap**·pi·er
un·**hap**·pi·est
un·**hap**·pi·ly
un·**hap**·pi·ness
un·**hap**·py
un·**health**·y
un·**heard**-of
u·ni·corn
u·ni·cy·cle

unicycle

un·i·den·ti·**fi**·a·ble
un·i·**den**·ti·fied
u·ni·form
u·ni·formed

u·ni·**form**·i·ty
u·ni·fi·**ca**·tion
u·ni·fied
u·ni·fies
u·ni·fy
un·im·**por**·tance
un·im·**por**·tant
un·in·**hab**·it·a·ble
un·in·**hab**·it·ed
un·in·**tel**·li·gi·ble
un·in·**ten**·tion·al
un·**in**·ter·est·ed
un·ion
u·**nique**
u·ni·sex
u·ni·son
u·nit
u·**nite**
u·nity
u·ni·**ver**·sal
u·ni·verse
u·ni·**ver**·si·ties
u·ni·**ver**·si·ty
un·**just**
un·**kind**
un·**known**
un·**less**
un·**like**
un·**like**·ly
un·**lim**·it·ed
un·**load**
un·**lock**
un·**luck**·y
un·mis·**tak**·a·ble

un•mis•**tak**•a•bly
un•**nat**•u•ral
un•nec•es•**sar**•i•ly
un•**nec**•es•sar•y
un•ob•**served**
un•**oc**•cu•pied
un•of•**fi**•cial
un•**pack**
un•**pleas**•ant
un•**pleas**•ant•ly
un•**plug**
un•**pop**•u•lar
un•pre•**dict**•a•ble
un•pre•**pared**
un•pro•**voked**
un•**pub**•lish•ed
un•**rav**•el
un•**rea**•son•a•ble
un•rec•og•**niz**•a•ble
un•re•**li**•able
un•**rest**
un•re•**strict**•ed
un•**ri**•valed
un•**roll**
un•**ruf**•fled
un•**rul**•y
un•sat•is•**fac**•to•ry
un•sci•en•**tif**•ic
un•**scru**•pu•lous
un•**seen**
un•**set**•tle
un•**set**•tled
un•**sight**•ly
un•**skilled**

un•**soc**•ia•ble
un•**sound**
un•**speak**•able
un•**sta**•ble
un•**stead**•y
un•suc•**cess**•ful
un•**suit**•a•ble
un•**sure**
un•**tan**•gle
un•**tan**•gling
un•**think**•a•ble
un•**ti**•di•ness
un•**ti**•di•ly
un•**ti**•dy
un•**tie**
un•**tied**

untied

un•**til**
un•**time**•li•ness
un•**time**•ly
un•to
un•**told**
un•**touched**

un•**true**
un•**ty**•ing
un•**used**
un•**u**•su•al
un•**wel**•come
un•**wield**•y
un•**will**•ing
un•**wind**
un•**wor**•thi•ly
un•**wor**•thy
un•**wound**
un•**wrap**
un•**wrapped**
un•**wrap**•ping
up
up•beat
up•bring•ing
up•**date** (v.)
up•date (n.)
up•**grade** (*or*
  up•grade) (v.)
up•grade (n.)
up•grad•ing
up•**heav**•al
up•**held**
up•**hill**
up•**hold**
up•**hol**•ster
up•**hol**•ster•er
up•**hol**•ster•y
up•keep
up•**on**
up•per
up•per•case

up•per **hand**
up•per•most
up•right
up•ris•ing
up•roar
up•**roar**•i•ous
up•**root**
up•**set** (v.)
up•set (n.)
up•**set**•ting
up•side **down**
up•stairs
up•stream
up•tight
up-to-date
up•ward
ur•**a**•ni•um

Ur•a•nus
  also pronounced
  Ur•**a**•nus
ur•ban
urge
ur•gen•cy
ur•gent
urg•ing
u•rin•ar•y **sys**•tem
u•ri•nate
u•rine
urn (sounds like
  "earn")
  *We saw a large Greek
  urn in the museum.*
us
us•age

use
used
use•ful
use•ful•ness
use•less
us•er-**friend**•ly
ush•er
us•ing
u•su•al
U•tah
u•**ten**•sil
u•ter•us
u•**til**•i•ties
u•**til**•i•ty
u•ti•lize
ut•most
U-turn

va•can•cy
va•cant
va•**ca**•tion
vac•ci•nate
vac•ci•**na**•tion
vac•**cine**
vac•u•um
vague
vain (sounds like
  "vane" and "vein")
  Vain people always
  think about
  themselves.
val•e•dic•**to**•ri•an
val•en•tine
Val•en•tine's **Day**
val•iant
val•id
val•i•date
va•**lid**•i•ty
val•ley
val•or
val•u•a•ble
val•u•a•bles
val•ue
val•ues
valve
vam•pire
van
van•dal
van•dal•ism
van•dal•ize

vane (sounds like
  "vain" and "vein")
  The weather vane
  shows which way the
  wind blows.
va•**nil**•la
van•ish
van•i•ty
va•por
var•i•a•ble
var•i•ant
var•i•**a**•tion
var•ied
var•ies
va•**ri**•e•ties
va•**ri**•e•ty
var•i•ous
var•nish
var•y (sounds like
  "very")
  Apples vary in size.
vase
vas•sal
vast
vast•ness
vat
vault
VCR
veal
veer
veg•an
veg•e•ta•ble

veg•e•**tar**•i•an
veg•e•**ta**•tion
ve•hi•cle
veil
vein (sounds like
  "vane" and "vain")
  This vein carries blood
  to the heart.
Vel•cro
ve•**loc**•i•ty
vel•vet
ven•**det**•ta
vend•ing
ven•dor
ve•**ne**•tian **blind**
Ven•e•**zue**•la
ven•geance
Ven•ice
ven•i•son
ven•om
ven•om•ous
vent
ven•ti•late
ven•ti•**la**•tion
ven•ti•la•tor
ven•tri•cle
ven•**tril**•o•quist
ven•ture
ven•ture•some
ven•tur•ing
ven•ue
Ve•nus

ve•**ran**•da (*or*
  ve•**ran**•dah)
verb
ver•bal
ver•dict
Ver•gil (*or* **Vir**•gil)
ver•i•fi•**ca**•tion
ver•i•fied
ver•i•fies
ver•i•fy
Ver•**mont**
Ver•**sailles**
ver•sa•tile
ver•sa•**til**•i•ty
verse
ver•sion
ver•sus
ver•te•bra (sing.)
ver•te•brae (pl.)
ver•te•brate
ver•ti•cal
ver•y (sounds like
  "vary")
  She is very tall.
ves•sel
vest
vet
vet•er•an
vet•er•i•**nar**•i•an
vet•er•i•nar•y
ve•to
ve•toed
ve•toes
ve•to•ing

vi•a
vi•a•**bil**•i•ty
vi•a•ble
vi•a•duct
vi•brant
vi•brate
vi•brat•ing
vi•**bra**•tion
vice (sounds like
  "vise")
  Cheating is a vice.

Viking

vice pres•i•dent
vice ver•sa
vi•**cin**•i•ties
vi•**cin**•i•ty
vi•cious
vic•tim
vic•tim•i•**za**•tion

vic•tim•ize
vic•tim•iz•ing
vic•tor
vic•to•ries
vic•**to**•ri•ous
vic•to•ry
vid•e•o
vid•e•o•cas•**sette**
vid•e•o•tape
vie
vied
Vi•**en**•na
Vi•et•**nam**
view
view•point
vig•i•lance
vig•i•lant
vig•or
vig•or•ous
Vi•king
vile
vil•la
vil•lage
vil•lag•er
vil•lain
vil•lain•ous
vil•lain•y
vin•**dic**•tive
vin•**dic**•tive•ness
vine
vin•e•gar
vine•yard
vin•tage
vi•nyl

vi•**o**•la

vi•o•late

vi•o•lat•ing

vi•o•**la**•tion

vi•o•**la**•tor

vi•o•lence

vi•o•lent

vi•o•let

vi•o•**lin**

vi•per

Vir•**gin**•ia

vir•tu•al•ly

vir•tu•al re•**al**•i•ty

vir•tue

vir•tu•**o**•so

vir•tu•ous

vi•rus

vi•sa

vise (sounds like
  "vice")

  *Put the wood in a vise
  before you saw it.*

vis•i•**bil**•i•ty

vis•i•ble

vis•i•bly

vi•sion

vis•it

vis•it•or

vi•sor

vis•ta

vis•u•al

vi•su•a•li•**za**•tion

vi•su•a•lize

vi•tal

vi•**tal**•i•ty

vi•ta•min

vi•**va**•cious

viv•id

viv•id•ness

vo•**cab**•u•lar•ies

vo•**cab**•u•lar•y

vo•cal

vo•cal **cords**

vo•cal•ist

vo•**ca**•tion

vo•**cif**•er•ous

vogue

voice

voice•print

voic•ing

void

vol•a•tile

vol•a•**til**•i•ty

vol•**ca**•no

vol•**ca**•noes (*or*
  vol•**ca**•nos)

vol•ley

vol•ley•ball

volt

volt•age

vol•ume

vo•**lu**•mi•nous

vol•un•tar•y

vol•un•**teer**

vom•it

vote

vow

vow•el

voy•age

voy•ager

vul•gar

vul•ner•a•**bil**•i•ty

vul•ner•a•ble

vul•ture

vy•ing

wack•i•er

wack•i•est

wack•i•ness

wack•y

wad

wad•dle

wad•dling

wade

wad•er

wad•ing

wa•fer

waf•fle

waf•fling

waft

wag

wage

wa•ger

wagged

wag•ging

wag•ing

wag•on

waif

wail (sounds like "whale")

The baby will wail when her mother leaves.

waist (sounds like "waste")

He has a 32-inch waist.

wait (sounds like "weight")

Wait for me!

wait•er

wait•ress

waive (sounds like "wave")

Did he waive his right to a lawyer?

(walrus)

waiv•ing

wake

wak•ing

walk

walk•er

walk•ie-**talk**•ie

walk•o•ver

walk•way

wall

wal•la•bies

wal•la•by

wal•let

wal•lop

wal•low

wall•pa•per

wal•nut

wal•rus

waltz

wam•pum

wand

wan•der

wane

wan•gle

wan•gling

wan•ing

want

war

war•ble

war•bler

ward

war•den

ward•robe

ware•house

wares (sounds like "wears")

There are wonderful wares to purchase here.

war•fare

war•i•ly

war•like

warm
warm-blood•ed
warm•er
warm•est
warmth
warn (sounds like "worn")
Warn him of the danger.
warp
war•rant
war•ran•ty
war•ri•or
war•ship
wart
war•y
was
wash
wash•a•ble
wash•er
wash•ing ma•chine
Wash•ing•ton
was•n't
wasp
waste (sounds like "waist")
What a waste of time!
waste•bas•ket
wast•ed
waste•ful
waste•ful•ness
waste•land
wast•ing
watch

watch•dog
watch•ful
watch•ful•ness
wa•ter
wa•ter•col•or
wa•ter•cool•er
wa•ter•cress
wa•ter•fall
wa•ter•front
wa•ter•ing
wa•ter•logged
wa•ter•mark
wa•ter•mel•on

watermelon

wa•ter **pis**•tol
wa•ter•proof
wa•ter•shed
wa•ter-**ski**
wa•ter-**skied**
wa•ter-**ski**•er
wa•ter-**ski**•ing

wa•ter•tight
wa•ter•way
wa•ter•wheel
wa•ter•works
watt
wave (sounds like "waive")
Surfers love a huge wave.
wave•length
wa•ver
wav•ing
wav•y
wax
wax•y
way (sounds like "weigh")
Which way to the elephant house, please?
we (sounds like "wee")
We are happy to be here.
weak (sounds like "week")
She was weak after her illness.
weak•en
weak•ling
weak•ness
wealth
wealth•i•er
wealth•i•est
wealth•y
wean

weap•on

weap•on•ry

wear

wear•i•er

wear•i•est

wear•i•ly

wear•i•ness

wears (sounds like "wares")

He wears green every Friday.

wea•ry

wea•sel

weath•er (sounds like "whether")

I like cold weather.

weath•er-beat•en

weath•er•ize

weath•er **vane**

weave (sounds like "we've")

She could weave a whole tapestry.

weav•er

weav•ing

web

web-foot•ed

wed

we'd (sounds like "weed")

We'd better be going now.

wed•ded

wed•ding

wedge

Wed•nes•day

wee (sounds like "we")

The wee man was an elf.

weed (sounds like "we'd")

I'll pluck that weed out of my garden.

week (sounds like "weak")

Next week I'm going to Texas.

week•day

week•end

week•lies

week•ly

weep

wee•vil

weigh (sounds like "way")

I weigh more than I did when I was born.

weighed

weight (sounds like "wait")

The weight of those boxes can break the table.

weight•less

weight lift•er

weird

weird•o

weird•os

wel•come

wel•com•ing

weld

weld•er

wel•fare

well

we'll (sounds like "wheel")

We'll have to see about that.

well-bal•anced

well-be•**haved**

well-be•ing

well-known

well-off

went

were (sounds like "whir")

They were there yesterday.

we're

weren't

west

west•er•ly

west•ern

West In•dies

West Vir•gin•ia

west•ward

wet

wet•land

wet•ter

wet•test

we've (sounds like "weave")

We've spoken about this before.

whack

whale (sounds like "wail")

We went on a whale-watching cruise.

whal•er

whal•ing

wharf

what

what•ev•er

what's

wheat

wheel (sounds like "we'll")

The wheel on my bike fell off.

wheel•bar•row

wheel•chair

wheel•ie

wheeze

wheez•ing

wheez•y

whelk

when

when•ev•er

where

where•a•bouts

where•as

wher•ev•er

wheth•er (sounds like "weather")

We will leave at 9 AM whether you're ready or not.

whew

which (sounds like "witch")

Which hat will you wear today?

whiff

while

whim

whim•per

whine

whin•er

whin•ing

whin•nied

whin•nies

whin•ny

whip

whipped

whip•ping

whip•poor•will

whir (sounds like "were")

The whir of the fan was loud.

whirl

whirl•pool

whirl•wind

whirred

whir•ring

whisk

whisk•er

whis•key

whis•per

whis•tle

whis•tling

white

White House

white•wash

whit•tle

whit•tling

whiz (*or* whizz)

whizzed

who

whoa

who'd

who•ev•er

whole (sounds like "hole")

You ate the whole pie yourself?

whole•sale

whole•sal•er

whole•some

who'll

whol•ly (sounds like "holy")

I am wholly satisfied with your grade.

whom

whom•ev•er

whoop

whoop•ing cough

whoop•ing crane

who's (sounds like "whose")

Who's responsible for this mess?

whose (sounds like "who's")

Whose skates are these?

why
wick
wick·ed
wick·er
wide
wide·spread
wid·ow
wid·ow·er
width
wife
wig
wig·gle
wig·gler
wig·gling
wild
wild·cat
wil·der·ness
wild·flow·er
wild·life
will
will·ful
will·ful·ness
will·ing
will·ing·ness
wil·low
wilt
wimp
win
wind (rhymes with
   "skinned")
*Do you feel
the wind?*
wind (rhymes with
   "kind")

*It's time to wind
down this game.*
wind-chill **fac**·tor
wind·mill

(**windmill**)

win·dow
win·dow·pane
win·dow-shop·ping
wind·pipe
wind·shear
wind·shield
wind·surf·er
wind·surf·ing
wind·swept
wind·y
wine
wing
wing·span
wink
win·ner

win·ning
win·ter
win·ter·green
win·ter·time
win·try
wipe
wip·ing
wire
wir·ing
wir·y
Wis·**con**·sin
wis·dom
wise
wish
wish·bone
wish·es
wisp
wis·**te**·ri·a
wist·ful
wit
witch (sounds like
   "which")
*The witch rode a
broomstick.*
with
with·**draw**
with·**draw**·al
with·**drawn**
with·er
with·**hold**
with·**in**
with·**out**
with·**stand**
with·**stood**

W

wit•ness
wit•ty
wives
wiz•ard
wiz•ar•dry
wob•ble
wob•bling
wob•bly
woe
wok
woke
wolf
wol•ver•ine
wolves
wom•an
wom•an•hood
womb
wom•bat
wom•en
won (sounds like "one")

We won the championship!

won•der
won•der•ful
won't
wood (sounds like "would")

Wood is an excellent building material.

wood•chuck
wood•en
wood•land
wood•peck•er

worm

wood•wind
wood•work
wool
wool•en
word
word•ing
word proc•ess•ing
word proc•es•sor
word•y
wore
work
work•a•ble
work•a•hol•ic
work•bench
work•book
work•er
work•man
work•man•ship
work•out
work•shop
work•sta•tion
world

World War I
World War II
world•wide
worm
worn (sounds like "warn")

This shirt is so worn it has holes in it.

worn-out
wor•ried
wor•ries
wor•ry
wor•ry•ing
worse
wor•ship
worst
worth
worth•less
worth•while
wor•thy
would (sounds like "wood")

I would like you to come.

would•n't
wound (rhymes with "crooned")

The doctor bandaged his wound.

wound (rhymes with "round")

He wound the clock every day.

wove
wran•gle

wran·gler
wran·gling
wrap (sounds like "rap")
Will you wrap my package?
wrapped
wrap·per
wrap·ping
wrath
wreak (sounds like "reek")
This twister will wreak havoc on the town.
wreath
wreck
wreck·age

wren
wrench
wres·tle
wres·tler
wres·tling
wretch
wretch·ed
wrig·gle
wrig·gling
wring (sounds like "ring")
Wring all the water out of your bathing suit.
wrin·kle
wrin·kling
wrist
wrist·watch

write (sounds like "right")
I'll write you every day.
writ·er
writ·ing
writ·ten
wrong
wrong·do·ing
wrote (sounds like "rote")
Shakespeare wrote great plays.
wrung
wry (sounds like "rye")
He has a wry sense of humor.
Wy·**om**·ing

Xe·rox
X ray (n.)

X-ray (adj. and v.)
xy·lo·phone

Y

yacht
yacht·ing
yak
yam
yank
Yan·kee
yap
yapped
yap·ping
yard
yard·stick
yar·mul·ke
yarn
yawn
year
year·book
year·ling
yearn
yeast
yell
yel·low
yel·low jack·et
Yel·low·stone
yelp
yen
yes
yes·ter·day
yet
Yid·dish
yield
yip

yipped
yip·ping
yo
yo·del
yo·ga
yo·gi
yo·gurt
yoke (sounds like "yolk")
The oxen shared a yoke.
yolk (sounds like "yoke")
Eat your egg yolk.
Yom **Kip**·pur
also pronounced **Yom** Kip·**pur**
yon·der

yo-yo

Yo·**sem**·i·te
you (sounds like "ewe")
I'm glad to meet you.
you'd
you'll (sounds like "Yule")
You'll see.
young
young·ster
your (sounds like "you're")
Here is your change.
you're (sounds like "your")
You're very welcome.
yours
your·self
your·selves
youth
you've
yowl
yo-yo
Yu·kon
Yule (sounds like "you'll")
I love the Yule season.
Yule·tide
yup·pies
yup·py

za•ny
zap
zapped
zap•ping
zeal
zeal•ot
zeal•ous
ze•bra
ze•nith
zeph•yr
zep•pe•lin
ze•ro
ze•ros (*or* ze•roes)
zest
zest•ful
Zeus
zig•zag
zig•zagged
zilch

zinc
zin•ni•a
Zi•on•ism
Zi•on•ist
zip
zip code (*or* ZIP code)

zebra

zipped
zip•per
zip•ping
zip•py
zir•co•ni•um
zith•er
zo•di•ac
zom•bie
zone
zon•ing
zoo
zo•o•log•i•cal
zo•ol•o•gist
zo•ol•o•gy
zoom
zuc•chi•ni
Zu•lu
Zu•ni
Zu•rich

Misspeller's Dictionary

Looking up a word can be really difficult if you get the first, or initial, sound wrong. Here are over 600 words with tricky beginnings. The word in the left column is the wrong spelling. Look in the right column for the right spelling.

Wrong Spelling	Right Spelling	Wrong Spelling	Right Spelling
chek	Czech	fizicist	physicist
chek	check	fizics	physics
chello	cello	fizique	physique
fantom	phantom	fizishun	physician
farmacist	pharmacist	flem	phlegm
farmacy	pharmacy	fobia	phobia
fase	phase	foenix	phoenix
faze	phase	fonetic	phonetic
feasant	pheasant	fonics	phonics
feenix	phoenix	fonograph	phonograph
fenomenal	phenomenal	fony	phony
fenomenon	phenomenon	fosforus	phosphorus
fezant	pheasant	fosphorus	phosphorus
filanthropic	philanthropic	fotocopy	photocopy
filanthropist	philanthropist	fotogenic	photogenic
filanthropy	philanthropy	fotografy	photography
filharmonic	philharmonic	fotograph	photograph
filodendron	philodendron	fotography	photography
filosopher	philosopher	fotojenic	photogenic
filosophy	philosophy	fraze	phrase
fizeek	physique	fysical	physical
fizical	physical	fysician	physician
fizician	physician	fysicist	physicist

Wrong Spelling	Right Spelling	Wrong Spelling	Right Spelling
fysics	physics	jenerous	generous
gage	gauge	jenesis	genesis
gastly	ghastly	jenetic	genetic
gerkin	gherkin	jenial	genial
getto	ghetto	jenie	genie
gliserin	glycerin	jenius	genius
gool	ghoul	jenocide	genocide
gost	ghost	jenra	genre
goul	ghoul	jenteel	genteel
heffer	heifer	jentile	gentile
hoo	who	jentle	gentle
hoom	whom	jentleman	gentleman
hoose	whose	jentry	gentry
hooz	whose	jenuine	genuine
jee	gee	jenus	genus
jeen	jean	jeodesic	geodesic
jee-wiz	gee-whiz	jeographic	geographic
jelatin	gelatin	jeography	geography
jem	gem	jeology	geology
jender	gender	jeolojic	geologic
jene	gene	jeometric	geometric
jeneologist	genealogist	jeometry	geometry
jeneology	genealogy	jeranium	geranium
jeneral	general	jerbil	gerbil
jeneralize	generalize	jeriatric	geriatric
jenerate	generate	jerm	germ
jeneration	generation	Jerman	German
jenerator	generator	jerminate	germinate
jenerosity	generosity	jerund	gerund

Wrong Spelling	Right Spelling	Wrong Spelling	Right Spelling
jesticulate	gesticulate	kache	cache
jesture	gesture	kackle	cackle
jiant	giant	kactus	cactus
jibber	gibber	kadet	cadet
jibberish	gibberish	kaf	calf
jibe	gibe	kafay	café
jigantic	gigantic	kaffeine	caffeine
jim	gym	kage	cage
jimnast	gymnast	kalf	calf
jimnastic	gymnastic	kalico	calico
jinger	ginger	kalipso	calypso
jinseng	ginseng	kall	call
jipsy	gypsy	kalligraphy	calligraphy
jiraffe	giraffe	kalliope	calliope
jist	gist	kalm	calm
jym	gym	kalorie	calorie
jymnasium	gymnasium	kalypso	calypso
jymnast	gymnast	kamel	camel
jymnastic	gymnastic	kamoflaje	camouflage
jypsum	gypsum	kampain	campaign
jypsy	gypsy	kampus	campus
jyrate	gyrate	Kanada	Canada
jyroscope	gyroscope	kanary	canary
kab	cab	kancel	cancel
kabbage	cabbage	kandelabra	candelabra
kabin	cabin	kandid	candid
kabinet	cabinet	kandidate	candidate
kable	cable	kandle	candle
kaboose	caboose	kandy	candy

Wrong Spelling	Right Spelling	Wrong Spelling	Right Spelling
kanine	canine	kardigan	cardigan
kanister	canister	kardinal	cardinal
kanker	canker	kardiograph	cardiograph
kannibal	cannibal	kare	care
kannon	cannon	kareer	career
kanoe	canoe	kareful	careful
kanoo	canoe	karess	caress
kanopy	canopy	karibou	caribou
kanser	cancer	karizma	charisma
kantalope	cantaloupe	karnation	carnation
kanteen	canteen	karnivore	carnivore
kantor	cantor	karpenter	carpenter
kanvas	canvas	karpet	carpet
kanyon	canyon	karrige	carriage
kaos	chaos	karrot	carrot
kapital	capital	kartilage	cartilage
kapitol	capitol	kartoon	cartoon
kapshun	caption	kartridge	cartridge
kapsule	capsule	karve	carve
kaptain	captain	kascade	cascade
kaption	caption	kashew	cashew
kaptivate	captivate	kashier	cashier
kaptive	captive	kaskade	cascade
kapture	capture	kasket	casket
kar	car	kasm	chasm
karacter	character	kassette	cassette
karamel	caramel	kastanets	castanets
karavan	caravan	kastle	castle
karbon	carbon	kasual	casual

Wrong Spelling	Right Spelling	Wrong Spelling	Right Spelling
katacomb	catacomb	koral	choral
katalog	catalog	korale	chorale
katalyst	catalyst	kord	chord
katapult	catapult	kord	cord
katastrophe	catastrophe	koreography	choreography
katch	catch	korus	chorus
kategory	category	krab	crab
katerpillar	caterpillar	kracker	cracker
kattle	cattle	kradle	cradle
kaucus	caucus	kraft	craft
kaught	caught	krag	crag
kauliflower	cauliflower	kramp	cramp
kauk	caulk	kranberry	cranberry
kaushon	caution	krane	crane
kavalcade	cavalcade	kranium	cranium
kavalier	cavalier	krank	crank
kavalry	cavalry	kranny	cranny
kavern	cavern	krape	crepe
kavity	cavity	krash	crash
kawk	caulk	krate	crate
kawt	caught	krater	crater
kazm	chasm	krave	crave
kemical	chemical	krawl	crawl
kemist	chemist	krawssant	croissant
kemistry	chemistry	krayon	crayon
klorine	chlorine	krazy	crazy
kloroform	chloroform	kreak	creak
klorophyll	chlorophyll	kreak	creek
kolera	cholera	kream	cream

Wrong Spelling	Right Spelling	Wrong Spelling	Right Spelling
krease	crease	krome	chrome
kreate	create	kromium	chromium
kredit	credit	kromosome	chromosome
kreek	creek	kronic	chronic
kreek	creak	kronicle	chronicle
kreem	cream	kronology	chronology
kreep	creep	krooked	crooked
krescent	crescent	krooze	cruise
kreviss	crevice	krop	crop
krew	crew	kross	cross
kricket	cricket	krouch	crouch
kriminal	criminal	krow	crow
kringe	cringe	krowd	crowd
kripple	cripple	krown	crown
kript	crypt	krucial	crucial
krisis	crisis	krucifix	crucifix
Krismas	Christmas	krude	crude
krisp	crisp	kruel	cruel
krissen	christen	kruise	cruise
krisskross	crisscross	krum	crumb
Krissmass	Christmas	krumble	crumble
kritic	critic	krumple	crumple
kriticism	criticism	krunch	crunch
kriticize	criticize	krusade	crusade
krochety	crotchety	krushal	crucial
krockery	crockery	krustacean	crustacean
krocodile	crocodile	krusty	crusty
krocus	crocus	kruze	cruise
kroissant	croissant	kry	cry

Wrong Spelling	Right Spelling	Wrong Spelling	Right Spelling
krypt	crypt	kwire	choir
krysalis	chrysalis	kwit	quit
krystal	crystal	kwite	quite
kwack	quack	kwivver	quiver
kwail	quail	kwiz	quiz
kwaint	quaint	kwoshunt	quotient
kwake	quake	kwota	quota
kwalify	qualify	kwote	quote
kwality	quality	kwotient	quotient
kwantity	quantity	nack	knack
kwarrel	quarrel	napsack	knapsack
kwarry	quarry	narl	gnarl
kwart	quart	nash	gnash
kwarter	quarter	nat	gnat
kwartz	quartz	nave	knave
kwash	quash	naw	gnaw
kween	queen	nead	knead
kweer	queer	nead	need
kweezy	queasy	nee	knee
kwell	quell	neel	kneel
kwench	quench	nell	knell
kwest	quest	nickerbockers	knickerbockers
kwestion	question	nife	knife
kwibble	quibble	nite	knight
kwick	quick	nite	night
kwiet	quiet	nob	knob
kwill	quill	nock	knock
kwilt	quilt	nockwurst	knockwurst
kwip	quip	noe	know

Wrong Spelling	Right Spelling	Wrong Spelling	Right Spelling
noe	no	rowt	rote
noll	knoll	salm	psalm
nome	gnome	sayder	seder
noo	gnu	sease	cease
nothole	knothole	seedar	cedar
notty	knotty	seenic	scenic
nowledge	knowledge	seiling	ceiling
nown	known	selebrate	celebrate
nu	gnu	selebrity	celebrity
nuckle	knuckle	selery	celery
numatic	pneumatic	selestial	celestial
numonia	pneumonia	sellar	cellar
onest	honest	sellar	seller
phantasy	fantasy	sellophane	cellophane
rack	wrack	sellular	cellular
rangle	wrangle	selluloid	celluloid
reath	wreath	sement	cement
reched	wretched	sene	scene
reck	wreck	sene	seen
reckage	wreckage	senery	scenery
reeth	wreath	sensur	censor
rench	wrench	sensur	sensor
restle	wrestle	sensorship	censorship
riggle	wriggle	sent	cent
rinkle	wrinkle	sent	scent
rist	wrist	sentennial	centennial
rite	write	senter	center
rong	wrong	sentigrade	centigrade
rowt	wrote	sentimeter	centimeter

Wrong Spelling	Right Spelling	Wrong Spelling	Right Spelling
sentipede	centipede	shuneel	chenille
sentral	central	shure	sure
sentrifugal	centrifugal	shute	chute
sentury	century	sider	cider
septer	scepter	sience	science
seramic	ceramic	sifer	cipher
sereal	cereal	sigar	cigar
seremony	ceremony	sigarette	cigarette
sertain	certain	silinder	cylinder
sertificate	certificate	sinch	cinch
sertify	certify	sinder	cinder
seudonym	pseudonym	sinema	cinema
shagrin	chagrin	sinic	cynic
shalay	chalet	sinnamon	cinnamon
shammy	chamois	sintillate	scintillate
shampain	champagne	sipher	cipher
shandelier	chandelier	sircle	circle
sharade	charade	sirculate	circulate
sharlatan	charlatan	sircumference	circumference
shateau	chateau	sircus	circus
shatoe	chateau	sissors	scissors
sheek	chic	sist	cyst
sheek	sheikh	sitadel	citadel
shef	chef	sitizen	citizen
shiffon	chiffon	sitrus	citrus
shivalry	chivalry	sivic	civic
showfer	chauffeur	sivil	civil
showvinist	chauvinist	sivilian	civilian
shugar	sugar	sivilization	civilization

Wrong Spelling	Right Spelling	Wrong Spelling	Right Spelling
sivilize	civilize	skorch	scorch
sizzors	scissors	skore	score
skab	scab	skorn	scorn
skald	scold	skotch	scotch
skale	scale	skoundrel	scoundrel
skallion	scallion	skout	scout
skallop	scallop	skowl	scowl
skalp	scalp	skowndrel	scoundrel
skamper	scamper	skraggly	scraggly
skan	scan	skram	scram
skandal	scandal	skramble	scramble
skant	scant	skrap	scrap
skar	scar	skrape	scrape
skarce	scarce	skratch	scratch
skare	scare	skrawl	scrawl
skarf	scarf	skrawny	scrawny
skary	scary	skream	scream
skatter	scatter	skreech	screech
skavenge	scavenge	skreen	screen
skedule	schedule	skrew	screw
skeem	scheme	skribble	scribble
skitzophrenic	schizophrenic	skrimmage	scrimmage
skoff	scoff	skript	script
skolar	scholar	skripture	scripture
skolastic	scholastic	skroll	scroll
skool	school	skrounge	scrounge
skooner	schooner	skrub	scrub
skoop	scoop	skruffy	scruffy
skooter	scooter	skruple	scruple

Wrong Spelling	Right Spelling	Wrong Spelling	Right Spelling
skrutinize	scrutinize	skwint	squint
skuba	scuba	skwire	squire
skuff	scuff	skwirm	squirm
skullery	scullery	skwirrel	squirrel
skulpt	sculpt	skwirt	squirt
skulpture	sculpture	skwish	squish
skum	scum	soodonim	pseudonym
skwabble	squabble	sychiatrist	psychiatrist
skwad	squad	sychic	psychic
skwadron	squadron	sychology	psychology
skwak	squawk	sycle	cycle
skwall	squall	syclist	cyclist
skwalor	squalor	syclone	cyclone
skwander	squander	syclorama	cyclorama
skware	square	sylinder	cylinder
skwash	squash	symbal	cymbal
skwat	squat	synic	cynic
skwaw	squaw	sypress	cypress
skweak	squeak	syst	cyst
skweal	squeal	sythe	scythe
skweamish	squeamish	terodactyl	pterodactyl
skweek	squeak	tomaine	ptomaine
skweel	squeal	wack	whack
skweemish	squeamish	wale	whale
skweez	squeeze	warf	wharf
skwelch	squelch	wat	what
skwib	squib	weat	wheat
skwid	squid	weaze	wheeze
skwiggle	squiggle	weel	wheel

Wrong Spelling	Right Spelling	Wrong Spelling	Right Spelling
weet	wheat	wiskey	whiskey
weeze	wheeze	wisper	whisper
wenn	when	wistle	whistle
Wenzday	Wednesday	wite	white
wether	weather	wittle	whittle
wether	whether	wiz	whiz
wich	which	woop	whoop
wich	witch	woosh	whoosh
wiff	whiff	wopper	whopper
wim	whim	wut	what
wimen	women	wy	why
wimper	whimper	yawt	yacht
wimsical	whimsical	zar	czar
wip	whip	zarina	czarina
wippersnapper	whippersnapper	zefer	zephyr
wippoorwill	whippoorwill	zenra	genre
wir	whir	Zerox	Xerox
wirlpool	whirlpool	zylophone	xylophone
wisker	whisker		

ABOUT THE AUTHOR

Marvin Terban's twenty books on the English language have been used to teach English as far away as China. He has won the Children's Choice award, and his *Scholastic Dictionary of Idioms* was named an American Bookseller "Pick of the Lists." A teacher of English, drama, and Latin, Mr. Terban lives in New York City.

PRAISE FOR OTHER SCHOLASTIC BOOKS BY MARVIN TERBAN:

Checking Your Grammar

Students will not have to wade through tedious or lengthy explanations to find what they need.... [This book is] attractive and so user-friendly that it can be read for fun.... *Grammar* illustrates the rules of proper grammar through nicely informal examples. The book also include chapters on sexist language, spelling rules, homonyms, and easily confused and misused words....   —*ALA Booklist*

There's a lot of grammar packed into this compact volume, and anyone who doesn't have a computer with spell check and grammar check needs it. Each of the three sections ("Building Sentences," "Parts of Speech," and "Style and Usage") is preceded by a detailed table of contents. Many necessary examples are provided. There is an index, but the excellent tables of contents are more useful. All in all, a handy guide.   —*School Library Journal*

Scholastic Dictionary of Idioms

...Fascinating.... This unusual work will intrigue children and may whet their appetites for other explorations of language.   —*Kirkus Reviews*

Terban explains the meaning and origins (if known) of more than 600 idioms and proverbs in this intriguing book.... Terban has obviously done a great deal of research.... A good resource for teachers who discuss idioms in the classroom....   —*ALA Booklist*

Reference tools may be a dime a dozen in this dog-eat-dog world, but here's a soup-to-nuts dictionary of colloquialisms that doesn't beat around the bush.... The sheer volume of examples...makes this an appealing browse as well as a useful (and perhaps unique) resource for kids baffled by the intricacies of the English language.   —*The Bulletin of the Center for Children's Books*